THE CLUTTER
BREAKTHROUGH

THE CLUTTER BREAKTHROUGH

YOUR FIVE-STEP
SOLUTION TO FREEDOM
FROM CLUTTER FOREVER

By Kelli Wilson

The Yellow Rose Press
Orangevale, CA

The information contained in this book is intended to be educational and is not intended to resolve disorganization due to AD/HD or Brain Injury where it has been diagnosed by a physician. This book is sold with the understanding that neither the author nor publisher is engaged in rendering any legal or psychological advice.

A portion of the proceeds from this book will be donated to the American Cancer Society in honor of Edna Jurgensmeier.

ISBN 978-0-9826405-0-0

Cover concept by Lisa Dalton
Cover design by Bourn Creative
Editing by Martin Sway
Book layout by Integrativeink.com

Printed in the United States of America

To Bailey and William who make me want to be a better Mom, woman and human being. I love being your Mom. I love you both!

Acknowledgements

To my Mom, Marlene and Step-Dad Don for all the love and support that made it possible for me to follow my dream. Thank you for loving me and my children the way that you do. I would not have been able to do it without you.

To my Dad, George, who is always there reaching out and encouraging me. Your support means a lot to me. You made this book possible, thank you for trusting me.

To Jan and Ken Kister, beloved friends and God's angels. Blessings to Healing for Survivors in Fresno, CA. The love and dedication to your work has enabled me to become the woman I am today. You started me on the journey that has changed my life and the life of my children forever. I am a very grateful Starfish!

To my favorite Rock Star Business Coach, Lisa Dalton, for believing in me, encouraging me, challenging me, pushing me and for holding up the mirror so that I could see the truth and possibilities.

To the women in my life who have been there to hold me up, encourage me and love me just as I am: Vikki Hubbard, Kathy Nishimoto, Rhoda Keith, Doris Willits and Christine Giri. You ladies mean so much to me.

About The Yellow Rose Press

In honor of the life and death of my mom, Edna Jurgensmeier, I created The Yellow Rose Press to represent the truth, power and unconditional love she represented. This book would not be possible without her influence on my life from 1977, when she married my Dad, until her passing June 26, 2007. She was my cheerleader and still is today with her voice in my head and heart as I go about setting and reaching my goals. Even when she saw me going in the wrong direction, she loved me anyway and was there to lift me up on the other side.

Breaking Through

Underneath it all is a burning truth
that we mistakenly believe is extinguished
But regardless of how dim the light
or dark the times
the truth can be rekindled
to the bright, beautiful
original light
for it was never really out
only buried beneath the
untruths allowed to hide it
Trust that everything is in perfect order
and that the light will shine again
Willingness fuels hope fuels trust fuels truth
believe in yourself and
truth outshines
everything else

Kelli Wilson

A Special note from the Author

I'm sharing a personal story with you in this book for two reasons: some of you will relate and need to know there's hope, and I believe it's relevant to the subject matter. My hope is that my transparency with the subject matter serves a greater purpose that I am sure I will never fully understand.

Introduction

Do you find yourself isolated in your home with your stuff, too afraid to let it go, too ashamed to invite anyone in, immobilized by an indiscernible captor that holds you hostage in your clutter? Is your stuff closing in around you? Are you overwhelmed and depressed but don't know how you got here or how to emerge? Maybe you have children or a spouse who simply wish to eat a meal at the table, sleep in their own bed or invite friends over, but the clutter prevents them from doing so. Or perhaps you have a relationship that is crumbling due to your unwillingness to let go of the clutter.

Or are you like millions of men and women who work or own their own businesses, support their spouses in their careers, manage their rental properties, pay the bills at home and take care of the house? Do you hurry the kids through their morning routines, drop them off at school and bring them back home, just to scramble back to the kitchen to cook dinner and do the dishes? Perhaps you sit on the board of the PTA or other professional association and attend networking functions to grow your business. You're constantly on the go and frazzled. Your desk is piled high, the laundry even higher, you rarely take care of yourself, and you shop to try to feel better.

Clutter and disorganization are your symptoms, the void inside of you that needs to be filled is the problem and the overall result is unmanageability—from the cluttered junk drawer to the inability to sustain relationships or commit to healthy sleeping habits. Within each of us exists this space that, if not naturally filled with good, nurturing self-acceptance, tends to fill with something else. The problem with filling it, or attempting to do so, with something external lies in the insatiable nature of the space. Some people try to fill it with drugs or alcohol, some fill it with food and others do so with romantic relationships. Then there are those who attempt to fill this space with *things*—retail therapy, a great sale, inheritance, valuable memorabilia—that, when taken to the extreme or done without real consciousness, makes life unmanageable.

The solution — the clutter breakthrough, takes us inside.

When I talk about going inside I'm talking about a spiritual journey. This isn't about religion, and I'm not telling you what to believe. Rather, this book is only the guide to help you find the truth that you have buried, which I will help you uncover if you're willing. Because we are talking about a spiritual process, we must talk about a power greater than ourselves, deep within ourselves, to which we can look as the guiding light. For some this is God. Others may look to Allah, Buddha, Source, Mother Nature or Universe. Regardless of what you call it, choose to invite Him/Her/It along on your journey, and allow yourself to depend on and trust that this awareness, this power, knows where you need to go. Yes, I said it! God. Call it what you'd like, but the key to healing is to believe there is a power greater than you that can help bring you to the peace you long for, fill the void and sustain that change. Throughout the book I will refer to this Power as God or Source, you may substitute your own word for God as you go.

This program is for you if

❑ you are willing to be uncomfortable in order to break through the clutter

❑ you are open to a spiritual solution to clutter

❑ you are willing to dig a little deeper

❑ you are committed to finding your own answers

❑ you are committed to walking through the truth

❑ you are ready to invest time in yourself

❑ you are willing to see your own value

There is no perfect adherence to this process! Don't create that kind of expectation. You do your best at any moment in time. Sometimes you can really progress, and sometimes you need to give yourself some care and compassion.

This is a universal solution to a specific problem. This is a solution that works as well as you apply it. These are very effective steps you can take to free yourself from the burden of clutter forever—not perfectly, not immediately—but definitely forever. You have to be ready to work at it, and work hard sometimes. How uncomfortable are you willing to be in order to free yourself from clutter? How willing are you to look at what you've been covering up for all these years?

You must be willing. And when you don't even have the willingness, you must be willing to be *willing*. Sometimes we have to start with being willing in order for the opportunities to present themselves and the process to begin. Know that your healing began long before you became consciously aware of it. That nagging discontent has been there, and it has led you inexorably to this point. Know that everything you experience in life leads you to each moment of decision. Now is a critical decision point.

Right now is the time to decide to
move forward and heal.

Welcome to the Solution!

Kelli Wilson

The Truth about the Stuff

Before we delve into the concepts and activities in this book, let us briefly discuss the truth about clutter and disorganization. The truth is, it's almost never about the stuff. Clutter in the case of the "collector," the "might need it later," the "it was a gift from family, so I have to keep it," the "I love it and can't do without it" or "it's not mine" is where this book applies.

If you find yourself saying any of the statements above, or if you are willing to consider finding yourself in the statements above, then you are on your way. This book is not for the person who *needs* it. There are millions upon millions of people who are using stuff to try to feel better. This book is for the person who *wants* it and is willing, or at least willing to be willing, to apply the slight, persistent effort necessary to recover from the effects of clutter and disorganization.

The truth is that these statements are the things we tell ourselves to keep from examining what's really behind the clutter and disorganization. Is it true that you might need something later? Absolutely. Is it true that you could have a gift from your family that you want to keep? Certainly. Is it true that the clutter can belong to someone else?

Sure. These are all possible truths. The determining factor is the effect the stuff is having on your life. If you might need it later and it doesn't adversely affect your life, then perhaps it's not an issue. If you're keeping a few manageable items from the family...okay. But a garage, a spare room, a back patio crammed full of stuff, overwhelming or defeated feelings, an unmanageable life...then we need to have a different conversation.

Although you may be certain you have an issue and you may already know it's deeper than the stuff, here are a few questions to consider for those of you that are still not convinced. Check all that apply.

❑ Do you sleep somewhere else other than your bed due to clutter?

❑ Do you consistently pay late fees because you don't have a mail and bill pay system that works?

❑ Are you chronically late because of the last-minute hunt for what you need to get out the door?

❑ Do you avoid having family and friends over due to the clutter in your home?

❑ Do you have to move things in order to sit down in your living room or at the kitchen table?

❑ Do your children miss out on having friends over or sleep over due to clutter?

❑ Do you park outside because the garage is full of stuff?

❑ Are you financially affected due to overbuying, late fees or mismanaged bills?

Each of these questions individually may reveal the presence of a greater issue. This is only a sampling of the list of symptoms that demonstrate how our external environment is a reflection of our internal environment.

A Little More about the Space

There are countless causes for the opening of that void. I cannot diagnose them, nor do I believe it's my job to. My intention is to guide you to peer into that space and look around to see what's really going on. Then I will be able to help you identify what can be changed in order to yield a different result in your life. After all, we cannot expect different results unless we take different actions.

The journey through my own space revealed some startling truths that I was hanging on to that were no longer relevant in my life. I've done a lot of work to free myself from the false truths of others and false truths of my society. Ultimately, I began to develop my own truths, which I hope this book guides you to do.

Through these concepts, and at your own pace, we will extract some of your truths, hold them up to the light of knowing and either keep them or replace them with a truth that better fits you and the direction in which you wish your life to move.

Some people may have grown up in a chaotic, unpredictable home, so they, at some level, derive security from the familiarity in that chaos. Taking their stuff away only leaves them feeling lost and scared. Perhaps that person had a traumatic experience and needs to be surrounded by stuff to feel safe. Similarly, stripping their stuff away from them may leave them feeling vulnerable. Or maybe that person suffered emotionally and uses clutter as a barricade to keep others at bay. I don't know what your space is about. That is for your discovery, your exploration, your inner work. What I do know is that you *will* find some answers so long as you stick to this program.

Removing the clutter isn't what opens you up to feel safe; rather, it needs to be done in tandem with inner work.

Why it doesn't work....

In the many years I have studied addiction, I have seen the best of intentions, the greatest desire to get better, fail. I have watched those with incredible emotional and spiritual pain remain trapped in their suffering, and I have seen people relapse because they lacked the resolve to do the necessary work. I have seen the skeptics who say spiritual work or therapy or this therapist or that psychologist didn't help. I have seen very slow progress and very quick forward momentum.

From my own experience of healing from childhood abuse—after many years of filling that void with people, places and things—I learned that it isn't linear working, it isn't "thinking" work, nor is it that *knuckle down, force a solution and move on with your life* kind of work: It is multilevel mental, physical and spiritual work. Let me emphasize the *work*.

This is where the external perception that people have about those who "can't get it done," can't stop drinking, can't stay clean, can't stop overeating, can't quit accumulating stuff, reaches the danger point. People who don't understand the many layers of addiction can easily misjudge those afflicted as lazy, stupid or not trying hard enough. A dance then begins between the afflicted and the loved one who wants them to just stop and get better. The family feels they are being put second to the clutter, so they become resentful, angry, sad—a large range of emotions—all while still loving the person who is struggling.

Awareness is always the first step in making any emotional, mental or spiritual change. This usually comes in the wake of great discomfort, sometimes from an ultimatum from a loved one, a change in health, losing the children or your home, or maybe it's that the resulting isolation has become too much. It is this tremendous discomfort that finally spurs us into action.

Throughout my childhood, I alone bore the burden of my abuse. I knew I couldn't tell anyone, but I didn't know it was ruling every decision I made and every thought I had about myself. My own value and self-esteem were nill. My decisions were based on the fear that, once again, I would be left there alone. Finally at 18, I told my boyfriend. He asked me questions like he already knew the answers, as if he knew that if I just told someone it would begin to get better and if he didn't resolve to draw the answers out of me they would slip back into the abyss where they had dwelled and believed it was my fault. I finally surrendered to the shameful truth and told him what they had done. People talk about the weight of the world being lifted: I felt a physical change in me at that moment in time, truly the weight of the world lifting. That was a powerful moment, but it would be another four years before I would began my most life-changing healing work.

Why is this story important? Because the process and time frame for your own healing journey are on no one but the spirit and soul inside of you. It's your journey. It's your process. It's your time. Many people endure great pain to free themselves and break the cycle. Others can only become aware but remain frozen by the fear of change. Some never see another possibility other than how their life looks and feels today. Some don't even realize that life would be better if they just discarded the notion that happiness, bliss, joyful serenity and a gratifying life are for everyone but them.

All of this is true and possible; all is the choice of the person and the spirit. I believe it's the journey of the soul and that it is all perfect. It's our judgment and the judgment of others that makes it not okay. As human beings, we subscribe to the notion that we are supposed to grow up, go to school, get a job, contribute something useful to society, retire and die. What if there's more to it? What if it all serves a greater purpose?

What if the hoarder is there to teach *us* something? Perhaps we can learn compassion and gain a deeper understanding of the need to fill the void. What if the guy sleeping in the doorway is there to teach us to be grateful for what we have—our mental and physical health—and to be aware that he is on his own journey. We need not judge that. What if the food addict is there to show us the importance of filling the void with love and spirituality rather than shorten our lives and endanger our health by doing so with food? What if we had compassion for their pain rather than judging their size? So the message here is to be gentle with yourself on this journey. Know that it is yours and that you are always right where you need to be. Like those mentioned above, others may judge and criticize *you*. Throughout this book you will find statements accompanied by a picture of a post-it note. When you see them I encourage you to scribble the statement on a post-it note and paste it on your bathroom mirror or throughout your home, car etc. This first one is about judgment, whether it be self-judgment or judgment from others.

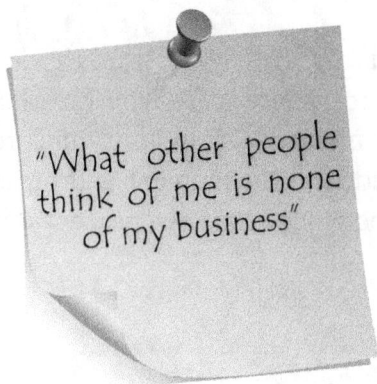

"What other people think of me is none of my business"

Be kind to yourself. You are your most scrutinizing critic, your harshest judge; you are the greatest obstacle to successfully liberating yourself from clutter and disorganization. Whether your inner critic tells you "you can't do it" and subconsciously you set out to validate that belief or you fear the feelings that will surface if you look at how clutter is serving you, you are the one who will ultimately decide to emerge or not.

So do this with me right now. Whether you are reading an online or a printed version, I want you to set it aside for a moment. Sit back in your chair so that you can feel the chair on your back and bottom. Put both feet on the floor and take anything out of your lap that you may be holding. Place your hands in your lap and drop your shoulders. Read the next few lines, then close your eyes and do it.

I am whole and complete

I am happy and calm.

Our minds are so complex it takes a lot of discipline and practice to silence it. As you breathed I hope you experienced a moment of tranquility and presence. When we are grounded in the moment and present in our life we get to experience calmness, peace and knowing.

A Note about Situational Disorganization

Situational disorganization occurs when a person deals with a major change or life event—loss of a loved one, a new baby, downsizing or relocating, retirement—and their lives are thrown into a state of temporary disarray. In cases of situational disorganization, a person may need only a gentle nudge to get back on track, as the temporary nature of this condition implies that the person was at one time organized.

A normally-organized person can find him or herself overwhelmed, for instance, when confronting the task of moving a four-bedroom house to two bedrooms. Perhaps a highly regimented woman finds the addition of a baby a challenge to her organization and routine. Or, perhaps, the death of a loved one leaves a person with too much to do in the midst of grief and mail and paperwork, and normal purging takes a back seat.

These situations may require some help, but with support from family and friends, order is gradually restored to your life. This book can help with situational disorganization. However, it is designed more to work for those who have persistent challenges with organization.

For the Family

This section is written with love and compassion to the family members of the people challenged by clutter, or even more, clutter addiction or hoarding. It's baffling at times to watch a loved one become absorbed in their stuff. If we've grown up in it but have adopted a more simple lifestyle today, it can be difficult to understand why our loved one still seems stuck in the clutter.

You may have chosen the other end of the spectrum and you've devoted yourself to minimalism. If you grew up with a family who collected, shopped or saved, it can be surfacing in a variety of ways in your own life today. You may also be a collector. Perhaps your parents' love was demonstrated by what they could give you materially, and consequently, you've valued yourself based on your possessions. Perhaps your parents and grandparents were influenced by the Depression when being thrifty and saving were a means to survive. Perhaps you were teased for living in squalor; perhaps you often dreamt of just having a family meal at the table where the surface was exposed. Maybe you resented never being able to invite a friend to visit or stay over. Or perhaps you experienced early on an event that created inside of you that space you so desperately attempt to fill.

Regardless of how you live your life in comparison to your loved one, how they live and how they evolve over the course of this program can still be confusing. You may see changes in them—sometimes consistent, sometimes not—that appear to be worsening rather than improving.

It is important to understand, as it has been explained throughout this book, that this is a process—a transformative journey—not a quick fix.

The person working through this program will be exploring themselves in relation to their spiritual, mental and physical self. They'll be asking themselves questions about their relationship to their stuff, and they'll be looking at their interactions and relationships to others in their life. It's important that you know this and understand that this is all new territory for them as much as it is for you watching them go through it.

Our greatest challenge, as humans, in relationships, is communication. No matter what your level or quality of communication is now, you are likely to experience some changes in this area. This could be more clear and honest communication from your loved one or a reduction in communication for a period of time—long or short—while they reflect on the work they are doing.

Patience...the good news is that you too can be looking at what is happening to your loved one and your relationship to them through your own set of lenses. Even if you are not a clutterer, you can treat these steps as universal and explore your own life. Replace the word *clutter* with anything and you can find your own answers. Maybe, for you, there is too much focus on what your loved one is doing, or not doing, and you could benefit from stepping back and taking care of yourself for a while. This book will walk you through how to do that. Not only will you better understand yourself and how you feel, but your feelings will change about the clutterer in your life too. If you are living with a clutterer, you can use the information in this book to look at how clutter and disorganization are affecting you directly. Is it painful to watch a loved one struggle? How are you contributing to the issues? Are you enabling the behavior?

I encourage you to take this opportunity to look at your own challenges. With willingness, communication and your own perspective, perhaps you can then work with your loved one to create the life you both desire. You deserve that.

Clutter Addiction

In his book, *The Addictive Personality*, Craig Nakken talks about addiction at its most basic level as an attempt to control and fulfill a desire for happiness. He talks about the human desire for peace and happiness and the natural cycle of life that occurs where peace may temporarily slip away; it's not wrong, it's just how life works. When change occurs, it can induce the grief process, which is a natural process that can vary in degrees. For some, they can go with the flow, and the pain of grief can be handled, felt and moved through. For others, they experience more extreme feelings and tend to want to hurry through the discomfort of the process. In their effort to alleviate the pain they may "self-medicate;" the "medication" could come in the form of alcohol, drugs, shopping, sex or gambling.

What does *breaking through the clutter* mean? This means that your decisions and thoughts are no longer dependent on shopping, spending, getting stuff, moving stuff around or feeling overwhelmed by clutter. It means that your life is no longer unmanageable because you can't breathe deeply under the weight of all your stuff. This is not about getting rid of the physical clutter as much as it is about releasing you from the hold it has on your life. This is not as much about what you acquire as it is about why you feel you *need* to acquire. Freedom from clutter is peeling away the layers of fear, emotion, memories and pain that feed the need for the clutter. You will no longer be dependent on the stuff in order to feel safe, fulfilled or complete. The truth is, that was only a temporary fix anyway. This book brings to light the possibility that you can fill yourself everyday with something that already exists inside of you. Like Dorothy who needed the journey to Oz to find her way back home, you too have already begun your journey back. You no longer have to search for the answers outside of you; you need only be brave and persistent enough to find them right within your heart.

> This is not about getting rid of the physical clutter as much as it is about releasing you from the hold it has on your life.
> – Kelli Wilson

How it works!

This book will only work for you if you work this book! There is no magic wand, no quick fix. The quickest way out is through, which is sometimes painful, but I guarantee it is worth the effort. If it were easy we would not have a clutter problem in America.

Achieving true freedom from clutter is not a single activity or engagement; it is a process that is less intense for some than it is for others. Finding freedom is a journey inward to understand how clutter and disorganization serve you and how to replace their purpose with a more organic, spiritual experience.

> The truth about
> clutter is that it
> takes you out of the moment.

We often want instant resolution to what challenges us, to what causes us pain or discomfort. You're probably reading this because your clutter and disorganization is somehow uncomfortable or costly to you. Perhaps a relationship is lost or you are financially affected as a result of misspending your money. Perhaps you have missed out on relationships or business opportunities because you cannot get places on time. You may be losing your job because you cannot focus on the tasks at hand due to clutter and disorganization in your office. Maybe your kids' academic performance is adversely affected by your inability to implement structure in their lives or your own. Or maybe you can't function in general because you are simply too overwhelmed.

Commit to diligently working on the concepts and questions in this book and you will find clarity and help for what challenges you.

Here is another affirmation to encourage you along your journey. Place it in your home or office to support you in the changes you are making.

> FREEDOM: The state of being free or at liberty rather than in confinement; the power to determine action without restraint; exemption from an unpleasant or onerous condition.

Freedom, by its very definition, is the act of releasing ourselves from the bondage of that which keeps us from living the life we were meant to live. Following are the steps we are going to take to break through the clutter.

The Clutter Breakthrough: Your Five-Step Solution to Freedom from Clutter Forever

1. ACKNOWLEDGE – HONESTY, HOPE & FAITH

You can't change what you are not willing to acknowledge. The most momentous step is the first, in which you acknowledge that there is a problem, especially when our self-preservation instincts tells us it is okay to ignore it and to prolong the denial. The following steps, however, are not necessarily linear. Rather, this is a cyclical process in which we often work on some area of our growth as best we can at that time only to come back around again later. Just keep in mind that every action is moving you forward whether you realize it or not.

It is important to know that you don't have any power over the clutter—otherwise you'd be done with it—but you do have power over your attitude and the ability to make choices. Attitude is everything. It may not seem like we have control over our attitude and emotions, especially anger, but they are ultimately choices that are made every day. After all, positivity is a choice, not a coincidence. Here are a couple of truths about attitude: What you focus on grows, and if you believe you can't, you can't.

What you focus on grows!

2. INVESTIGATE – COURAGE & INTEGRITY

In this step we will look into the areas of our life and investigate the space. Some truths, often deeply buried, may not be immediately revealed; hence we proceed in the cyclical manner discussed in step one. In doing so, we slowly and courageously peel back the layers—the proverbial onion—and peer inside. Peeling them all back at once would be overwhelming, but by completing the steps in the order in which they are prescribed, emerging from your situation will be less overwhelming and less frightening, so long as you have a strong foundation.

3. RELEASE – WILLINGNESS & HUMILITY

This step is about relinquishing the burdens of guilt and shame that separate you from God or Source, which in turn distance you from peace and serenity. This step is three-fold: spiritual, physical and mental. You will commence shedding the old beliefs, messages and stories you've been telling yourself, and you will begin to consider removing physical clutter. Removing items from the house goes hand in hand with the spiritual cleansing. They will feed each other, as the void previously occupied by a material possession can be filled with spirituality. You'll determine your refill routine, be it prayer and meditation or keeping a journal. You'll decide.

4. MAINTAIN ~ PERSEVERANCE & SPIRITUALITY

The previous steps have begun to clear the space inside of you of all the stuff keeping you disconnected from the moment. It is important to replace those things with daily spiritual practice. This doesn't have to be an elaborate process—simply connect each day with God. The better your connection and the more diligent you are in devoting yourself to this task each day, the more spiritually rewarding this work will be.

5. SHARE ~ BE OF SERVICE

Sharing your story—the more you give, the more you get—will surely lead you to one of life's most amazing paradoxes: You have to give it away to keep it. When you finally find a solution to what has been heavy in your heart for as long as you can remember, your own personal journey is greatly enriched by bestowing it to someone else. You may find that you are overflowing with good feelings as you continue through this work. I encourage you to share the feelings and your experiences with others.

> "You can have everything you want if you just help enough people get what they want"
> – Zig Ziglar

My Story

It was a family community—small houses, the streets buzzing with the chatter of children—where you played until the call to come home sounded or the street lights came on. The house was nestled in the middle of the block, and there was a tree growing in the big lawn that surrounded it. A little red rail fence separated it from the downhill neighbor. Its three bedrooms were sufficient for the young family of five. The boys shared a room; the girl had her own room at the beginning of the hallway. It was the perfect place to grow up. The backyard was large and grassy. When you came out the backdoor you could see a large area gated off for a garden. As you walked farther out onto the covered patio, you could see the square shed, just beyond it were raised rabbit cages.

It was near the rabbit cages and even in her own bedroom that things would be done to her by neighborhood boys that would create a space inside of her. This had happened to her before, but it was usually one-on-one: in the neighbor's house or in her own bedroom at night.

There was evidence that they had entered the house. The parents thought it was strange that the two-by-four piece of wood blocking entry through the back door was moved and the door left unlocked, but their initial alarm faded when they found nothing missing. The reason was because they had stolen her spirit—her soul, her voice, her dignity and her self-esteem. These things you can't see. They don't sit on a shelf or on the coffee table, and when they are taken away they leave behind a void, a space so large in the core of who we are that it seems impossible to fill.

"She" is me. And the space is created.

She is me thirty-five years ago. Some people set out, as I did, to fill that space with stuff or the love of all the wrong people. I learned at a very young age that my value hinged on the external world. It came from what I could do sexually, from how I could serve another regardless of how much it would cost me.

The life I experienced up until my parents' divorce created, in me, that ravenous space inside my spirit, at the core of who I am, which I then started out to fill throughout my life. I fell into that Jerry McGuire myth that, somehow, someway, someone outside of me was going to "complete me." It was those kind of messages fed my denial and fantasy.

I had not been present in my body—I mean *really* present—from the first moment I had to leave myself in order to endure the sexual abuse I suffered. From that first moment until today, as I'm writing, I have always had to be mindful about where I am in the moment. Am I back in the past, thinking I should've or could've done things differently? Or am I in the future thinking "I'm gonna..." or "if I just..." or "when I...," or am I *right here, right now* in the moment?

Back then, for me *right here, right now* was a really painful place to be. I had to reside in my own fantasy, as I wasn't equipped as a child, teen (God, help us with the hormones) or as a young adult to deal with being in the moment.

My decisions were based on fear and denial of reality, on filling that void inside me. It wouldn't be until many years later that I finally found the answers. I needed my life journey to bring me to this point where, today, I regret nothing—the abuse, the teen years—about my life. It has all prepared me for the purpose for which I am here today writing this book and for the message I must pass on to others.

I have to admit, my jobs I worked at served many purposes for me. From clothing stores to drug stores to Corporate America, my jobs served as a way to distract me from feeling. If I could only work more or maintain relationships just deep enough to be acceptable but never let them know the *real me*, then I was great. My work also served as a way for me to satisfy that space that needed approval, so I worked harder and longer than most. The catch was that I rarely knew what I was doing well enough to be great at it, but the sheer volume of it seemed to get me by. Then *he* came along...

I just knew that if he loved me enough, I would be okay; that if we had the right house, the right car, the best clothes, the great jobs, the ample income, I would be okay. I would finally be happy. We had a whirlwind relationship that could fill its own book, but, basically, I, once again, looked to someone else to make me complete, to fill the void. For some time he did it, but drugs and alcohol got in the way.

31

The first divine intervention in my life, that to this day I still cannot explain, happened: I moved away. I packed everything that would fit into my little blue Plymouth Champ, and I left. In January, 1989, I chose to live with my dad and stepmom in Fresno, California. I came from the San Francisco Bay area and settled in with my folks again at age 19. I can say that I have no idea to this day why I chose to move or where the strength came from to do it. I lived and breathed by the man I was "in love" with.

I found Healing for Survivors in Fresno and began my journey there. I attended weekly support groups and more than a dozen intensive weekend workshops to go back and clean up the pain of my past. **This process uncovered, over the course of a few years, the spiritual, emotional and physical numbness I had experienced** up to that point. The pain and disillusionment that ruled me all my life began to loosen its grip as I worked more and more on my abuse issues. It was to be a long process.

Healing for Survivors, an unassuming place whose impact in a person's life by far outshines its humble appearance, was started by Jan Kister, a woman whose passion for guiding others to healing was preceded only by knowing she had to do everything she could to help others break the cycle of abuse. I spent a year or two cleaning out the wounds that kept me stuck. My time at Healing for Survivors came to an end, but the journey onward took on a whole other life.

He came back and this time we got married and had two children. After all, we had both grown up quite a bit, and I convinced myself it would be different this time. Once again, I just knew if he loved me enough I would be okay. I just knew that if we had the right house, the right car, the best clothes, the great jobs, the ample income, I would be okay. I would finally be happy. Déjà vu!

Despite the fresh start and years of maturing, something still lingered inside of me: I was miserable, and I made everyone around me miserable too! Nothing I bought, did, traveled to or unwrapped made any difference...well...maybe temporarily, but nothing really endured. Believe me, I tried. We moved to the "nice" part of town, into a huge million-dollar home. Nope, still miserable.

Then, something happened. It had started to happen in between the births of my two children. See, I had been on a journey for many years by now to find out why I was unhappy, why my life didn't seem to work. I had uncovered a lot of the abuse and healed a great deal, but I was still blaming someone else. I wasn't ready to take responsibility for my own life and my own decisions, for the hole that was still inside of me that I was trying to fill with stuff and men. I thought "If you would just love me better I would be okay, if I could just have that, that new thing, I would be okay." One day I got it, intellectually. I finally realized that it's not about the stuff. But let me tell you, the journey between my head and my heart where it really resonates, is a million miles.

I arrived at this epiphany in November of 2001, when I began an introspective, spiritual journey to *try* yet another way to feel better. Up until this point I had enjoyed much success with Healing for Survivors, but I no longer lived in Fresno and I was at a standstill with traditional, sit-around-and-talk-about-it therapy, which was all I seemed to have access to.

By the time I conceded to the spiritual journey I wasn't even skeptical. I was too desperate to be skeptical. I just wanted to feel better, to be happy and not so angry. So my journey began. I immediately found someone to guide me, and we made some headway, but it wasn't the spiritual change that I craved. I couldn't even put the words to it. I just knew there was still something missing. I moved on, as we frequently do, to another person who helped me to peel back some very deep layers of shame and blame that were weighing me down.

By 2005, I had left my marriage and was a single mom, not part of my grand plan to "have it all." Nor was it the glamorous life I had envisioned as a girl. I was still waiting for Prince Charming to come whisk me away and take care of me, and I continued to seek him out in all the wrong places. Finally, as things always do, it happened: I experienced another divine intervention, one that would have a profound effect on the rest of my life.

Here's the divine part: I sat down next to a lady—with no intention of asking her to guide me prior to this moment in time—and leaned over and asked her if she would work with me. I don't know why. I didn't have the thought in my head at any time prior to that moment, but the words poured out of my mouth. I think I was as surprised as she was. She invited me to talk about what we could expect from each other and we immediately began working together.

Here's the thing: She has been practicing a spiritual lifestyle almost as long as I have been alive. She's twice my age and wise, wise, wise. I knew the moment we began talking that I was really going to work hard with her.

Today, I am a single woman at 41 with small children. The space inside of me that originated in sexual abuse and abusive relationship after abusive relationship is overflowing with the energy and spirit that comes from God, a power in my life that refills me, allowing me to be tireless in my service to others and that 'recalibrates' me when I am willing to see that I've wandered off track—God.

I think it's critical I share that, for me to move forward, I had to begin to forgive. I had to forgive myself, first and foremost, and I had to forgive those around me that I blamed for everything wrong in my life. For me, I had to look at what part I played in the steps that led me to this point and decide how I would resolve it within myself.

At five and six years old, I didn't have responsibility in my abuse, but today, I have a choice about how I will use it going forward. Once I became aware of how much the abuse affected the fiber of who I am, and once I found a place to go in order to begin healing, I became responsible for my abuse. What I mean is, I could let it continue to control my *every* decision—Make no mistake: It affected my decision-making because it affected my self-esteem—or I could decide to accept it as an opportunity to heal my spirit and help others.

When I decided to use it to benefit others, I began to learn that resentment and anger were in the way of the good my experience could serve. I had to dig through that pain in order to get to the place where I could share with others from a place of hope, humility, love and faith. Without the forgiveness I wouldn't have been able to do that. Don't get me wrong: It was some of the hardest work I did, but the more willing I was to do it, the more amazing, free and serene my life became.

Imagine seeing people in your life through the lens of love, acceptance and tolerance. For some of you reading this now you're thinking, "No way in Hell, never!" Others are thinking "You're crazy, lady!" Then there are those that are thinking, "Maybe, just maybe." I spent a lot of time in "Hell no" and that is okay. I accept today that things happen in perfect timing—not *my* perfect timing, but God's perfect timing. I believe we are here for our own spiritual growth, and as we do our own work, others reap the benefits.

Today I have a wonderful, loving relationship with my parents. They are incredibly supportive of me in everything I do. They are amazing grandparents, and my children are blessed with a safe place to grow up, just like the safe place I can now create and provide for them because I can love myself first. My parents had their own challenges growing up. I am able to see that, accept it and love them right where they are. What a blessing that is. I no longer look to them to do the impossible, make me happy or complete, or fill the space inside me.

It's God that fills the space for me.

This book is about finding out what fills the space for you. I hope you find your answers here, and I hope you learn that you are an amazing and valuable human being exactly as you are in this moment. My wish for you is that you gain all the love, peace and joy that I have found in my life through these steps.

Kelli

Step 1 - Acknowledge

The first step is to **Acknowledge**! You can't change what you won't acknowledge.

You're already on your way with this concept by simply having bought this book. You recognize that clutter and disorganization have taken over your physical, emotional, spiritual and mental space. You probably feel defeated, ashamed, depressed and exhausted, and you may continually try to convince yourself that it's not that bad, that there are others who are worse, that you want it this way or maybe you just don't have the time or energy to keep up with everything. All of this may be true at some level, but if you've picked up this book, there is something somewhere inside you that wants to do it differently, you just don't know how. Or maybe you know what you need to do but you just can't get yourself to do it or you do it but can't keep it that way. Somewhere inside you just know you want it to be better...

If so, you are in the right place. Know that we often have to step outside of ourselves and our comfort zones to grow and move beyond where we have been stuck for so long.

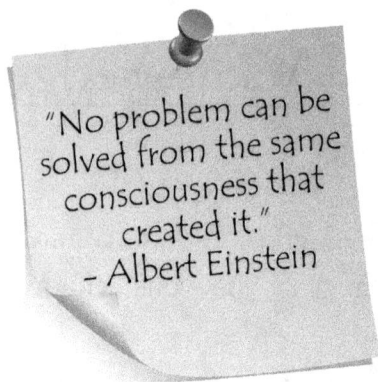

"No problem can be solved from the same consciousness that created it."
– Albert Einstein

Let's be clear right away. This is not a quick-fix book. Anything that creates enduring results requires a process that, for some, may be quick but for many can take more time to fully transform and become who we want to be.

I'm not talking about cleaning our closet or office and then following a maintenance plan. I'm talking about change at a deeper level, at a spiritual level. Earlier in the book we talked about the fact that it's not about the stuff. Here's where we begin to look inward with that statement and bring it directly to you. We're talking about addressing the issue at a spiritual level to create lasting change, about making the effort to better understand why things are the way they are and how to change them at a deeper level so that you can enjoy the results and have a richer life. Clutter and disorganization have taken over and this first step is about acknowledging that and deciding to begin the journey to find some relief from the control it's had over your life.

I'm not asking you to embrace this concept immediately, only to be willing to acknowledge that this is an area in which you are stuck. This means that all your good intention, thinking and desire haven't been sufficient to loosen you from the grip clutter has on your life. Your life is unmanageable and clutter is the symptom. You know this is true if you checked any of the boxes in the "Truth about the Stuff" section.

The process of this first step is really accepting and being willing to continue through this work with slight persistent effort. Be aware of any resistance you have to the idea that you are defeated by clutter, that your life is unmanageable. The attempts to manage your clutter, put it in pretty boxes and shuffle it around are exercises in futility unless you recognize it as your attempt to control your surroundings. There are standard organizing principles that call for sorting and boxing stuff up; however, there is a point in which this is no longer effective. When the stuff is boxed for the season, for tax documentation purposes or for legitimate archival purposes, this makes sense. But, if you can no longer invite people over because there is nowhere to sit, I would ask you to be willing to question yourself about that.

Here's what almost inevitably happens when this work begins (which is why the success rate for recovery from any addiction is so low): The truth begins to surface and all the survival methods we have used until this point go into overdrive and panic mode. Everything you have always known about how to manage and fill that abyss is fighting to remain true while a new idea is introduced. When we change it creates loss. When there's loss, there's grief.

The natural cycle of life is about change. That familiar quote, "The only thing we can count on is change," rings remarkably true. It's our **unwillingness** to accept that we are in a constant state of change that causes much of our struggle and pain. Even deeper than that is the fact that, with change, comes grief.

No matter how great or small the change—the death of a loved one, loss of a job, getting a new job, divorce, marriage or loss of a friendship—grief happens. When we dismiss or deny the natural process of grief we tend to compensate for the pain that wasn't dealt with.

Dr. Elisabeth Kubler-Ross first introduced the five stages of grief in her 1969 book, *On Death and Dying*, where she describes the process through which people deal with grief and loss. The five stages are denial, anger, bargaining, depression and acceptance. While Kubler claims these stages don't necessarily need to happen in this order, nor does everybody experience every stage, her book does bring to mainstream awareness the necessity to move through the grief. It is my experience that getting or remaining stuck in any one of these stages is where unmanageability begins. Whether it shows up as clutter or some other symptom, it can inhibit spiritual growth and happiness.

In his book, *The Addictive Personality*, Craig Nakken describes the addictive process as an attempt to manage the uncontrollable ebb and flow of emotions throughout our life experience. He writes that many of us strive for that peace of mind and soul and achieve it for periods of time. Sometimes it will slip away, but it returns. Nakken discusses that the addictive cycle begins when people use objects or substances to create the peaceful feeling of wholeness rather than accepting the process and letting it return naturally.

> This can be a never-ending cycle unless healing is sought.

The healing begins when we become willing to look at our relationship with stuff and what purpose it serves for us, when we become willing to really see how clutter and disorganization have taken us out of living in today. Addiction by its very nature takes us outside ourselves for answers that can only be found within. It causes us to lose sight of who we are and what our purpose is, and it sometimes quietly and slowly steals our life away without us even knowing it is happening.

This is not to say that every person who experiences the feelings described above is addicted, but it is worth exploring if your life has become unmanageable. *Unmanageable* has a different meaning for each person, but a couple of examples could be that accumulating and keeping takes priority over almost everything else in your life. You shop to fill the space and your home overflows with stuff. You shop to fill the void and your credit cards are maxed out or close to it, and you're paying the minimum payment. *Unmanageable* can also mean that your need to shop causes ongoing tension, anxiety or fighting in your relationships.

So the normal response to lifting the veil is fear and discomfort. The normal response to fear and discomfort is to soothe it just like you always have: shopping, collecting, sorting, moving or stirring up the chaos of clutter to keep from feeling the feelings. I'm asking you to become aware of just how clutter and disorganization serve you, to think about the ways clutter and disorganization perpetuates the chaos and drama in your life.

Clutter may be inanimate, but it has energy. Everything around us has energy. When the volume of stuff around us becomes overwhelming it affects how we feel and interact within our space, our ability to breathe deeply, to rest well and to move about freely. In extreme cases it can affect our health if there are large amounts of paper breaking down and becoming airborne, if pets or other critters are leaving excrement in our living space or if we cannot safely move about our house without stepping over things or moving things as we go. Clutter and disorganization don't need to win.

This program works with a variety of principles that will be defined in each step. The definitions of the principle will be spelled out, but I encourage you to look at what the words mean to you and how they are or are not showing up in your life today. As we move further along in the steps of this program, you'll revisit these principles and work to bring their benefits forward as you grow. You will change old beliefs, and the messages in your head will change about these principles.

Again, this is a process. You may find that it feels as if nothing has shifted. As I said earlier in the book, the transformation and work and changes may be happening at a level you cannot yet see or feel.

The absolute truth in this moment, as you read this, is that your life is unmanageable—that the clutter and disorganization have taken over in such a way that you are no longer able to make a decision that isn't influenced by clutter or what it covers up. I know what you're thinking: You're probably thinking this isn't true or that clutter and disorganization are not controlling what you do and feel. Or at least you're thinking, "Sure my house is a mess and I'm always late, but I have 'reasons' for that: He/she makes me late, or stuff happens outside of my control, so I can't help it." Or, "I am working full-time with three kids, each with three activities and homework and dinner and laundry and housework, so I can't help having a messy house."

I hear you. Stuff happens, and I really hear you about the responsibilities at home. I'm a single mom running my own business, I am a partner in another, I'm volunteering at school, writing a book, cleaning toilets and mowing lawns. I understand the responsibility and the overwhelming feelings that can show up in our lives. I also understand that there are some of you who are very right-brain oriented and that the nuts and bolts of organizing elude you. This book may not be for you. You may simply need someone to help you create systems that you can put into place to keep you on track. If you've done that once or several times and have not had lasting results, this book could help you uncover the resistance to change or resistance to sticking with the system that you started.

Sometimes it may be about just not wanting to conform and do what has been laid out to do. I have had clients who have plainly said, "If it's not my idea, I'm not doing it." In my opinion there's a deeper message there.

This book is so little about neat cupboards and perfect schedules; it deals more with using clutter and disorganization as an excuse for the state of your life. Clutter is not why your life is unmanageable; rather it's the symptom that your life is unmanageable, the secret you are carrying, the belief you have about yourself or others, or the truth you haven't dealt with.

This may be the first time you've heard this idea, that it's not about the stuff. If so, you may want to read through this section again. Otherwise, welcome back to the idea that there's another reason for unmanageability.

You may have heard it many, many times. What's different is that I'm calling you out to the truth about the stuff; the unmanageability; and the denial of how clutter, disorganization and unmanageability rule your life. The difference here is that I am giving you the road map to free yourself from the symptom of your unmanageability.

Failed efforts are there
for you to examine
and learn from.
— Kelli Wilson

Step by step you can do it, but you have to *do* it. You have to commit. **Failed efforts are there for you to examine and to learn from.** It's not always the right time, but you'll know when you are ready to do this work because even when it hurts to look at yourself, you'll still keep walking through. You would rather walk through and get better than remain, any longer, in the way your life works today. It takes courage to do this. You have it. You can do it.

Be cautious, however, about letting perfectionism— where you wait to begin until all the conditions are perfect—prevent you from starting. If perfectionism plays any part in your clutter and disorganization, be aware right now that it can be an excuse to continue putting off what you need to do to move forward. Decide that now is the time to try. Every time I take on a client who has been frozen in their stuff they ask, "Where do we begin?" I always respond, "We just do." Begin and let the process unfold. Trust that there is a plan outlined in this book, and if you just do the next thing outlined for you, you will make it through. It's not easy, as we've already discussed, but you're worth it and you can do it.

As I'm writing this book, I'm dealing with my own challenges with disorganization and perfectionism. I'm a very visual and kinesthetic person. Words on a page are often like a foreign language to me, even more so when I'm putting any of my own thoughts on paper that are more complex than a list. I have been lost many times in the process of writing this book, and it stopped me many times from moving forward, but my goals and accountability keep me on track. I have created that for myself because I know me, much like you know yourself:

I need someone to check in with, follow up with and to be accountable to. I used to feel shameful about this. Why couldn't I do it myself, just get it done? I know what needs to be done: Do the work, write the book, publish the article and call that client. This has given me even more passion for the message and compassion for the reader who struggles with this in almost every area of his or her life.

Through doing this process myself, I have learned that this is how I tend to work. I work well under pressure, with a deadline, and I work especially well when I know I have to report in. These qualities make me a great employee. However, when I launched my own business and set out to write this book, I had done enough of this work to know that I have to create a support system around me to have accountability and goals. I still have to do the work, but knowing me and how I show up really makes a difference in accomplishing my goals.

This is what this process is really all about: getting to know yourself better, the parts of you that you have tucked away and deemed unacceptable. You are not ugly and unacceptable; you are an amazing person. This process is about bringing those things back out and examining them under a different light, about allowing them to shine. When you find things that are no longer working in your life, you can begin to change them. This is where the miracles happen. We'll get there soon enough. This step is about getting to know yourself so you can really examine what is working and what is not.

I want you to know that I did this work. I have answered the questions I am about to ask you to answer. I have shared them with a trusted friend, and I have learned a lot about myself in the process. Now I share this with you because I want you to know that you can do it. It is a critical piece of the process, take your time and really honor it.

Are you ready to do the work?

Okay, come on out! I'm calling you out. Your family may have called you out in a variety of ways: in quiet conversation, in dramatic fashion, or they may have cleaned for you without your permission, creating resentment and distrust. They may be quietly suffering and feeling overwhelmed; I have a chapter for them in this book. You can read it yourself, and if you are comfortable, show it to them or buy them a copy of this book so they can see and begin to understand what you are doing.

Right now this is about you. I am asking you to take a risk, to trust, to be willing and to surrender to this process. I am asking you to look at yourself and to love yourself enough to allow this process to work you as *you* work *it*.

How uncomfortable are you willing to get to heal?
Our first principle is honesty.

> HONESTY: Free from fraud or deception; marked by free, forthright and sincere expression.
> (Webster online)

The honesty I'm talking about is an honesty that sometimes takes years to understand and integrate. It means seeing ourselves for who we really are, not as others see us, but as God sees us. It means that we become vulnerable to the idea of introspection and possibility. This does not mean complete vulnerability to the world; rather, it is being honest with yourself and God as a means to learn and grow. I'll give you the steps, but the power you choose will create the foundation on which you'll stand, and it will hold you up when you feel you can't do anymore. It's that spiritual power that will fill and sustain that space you have been attempting to fill with stuff.

I am not going to tell you who or what to choose or what to call it, but I am going to ask that you choose something. This something, I will continue to refer to as God or Source, becomes the "source" from which your strength, faith and serenity come from. Some people choose to reacquaint themselves with the God they grew up with; some people have been deeply wounded by people or events in their religious upbringing and have severed all attachments to God. If this is you, I would encourage you to redefine God. Rename God "It" if you must, but be willing to open yourself up to the possibility that there is some benevolent force out there that wants nothing more than to fill your life with serenity and joy. You may choose Mother Nature or a tree in your yard, or you may choose the energy and Source through which this book was brought to you. Regardless of what you call it—Universe, Allah, Buddha—feel that it is a safe and consistent source of strength for you while you continue through this self-exploration to freedom.

I grew up in organized religion going to church with my grandparents each Sunday. I loved it there. I was able to be a kid, which was difficult owing to the events of my life that aged me before my time. I started out in Sunday School and vacation bible school, and I felt good there because I knew what to do and what to expect. God was well-defined and the services were predictable, unlike my home. I needed to behave a certain way, and I loved consistently knowing what to expect. There were certain truths in that church that just weren't questioned, at least not at my young age. I never questioned it; it worked for me at the time.

I accepted it, though as I grew up and as my childhood bubbled up to try to find the sunlight of truth, I needed more than the rules and outlines. I needed more but wasn't really ready to redefine it, so I walked away from the church and from God. I always knew, at some level, that there was something inside of me that carried peace; I just lost the ability to connect with it for many years. I continued in search of the external solutions. I looked for "him" or "her" or for other things—a bigger house, nicer car, better paying job—to do the trick. Once I had all those I would finally be okay. When I began to apply these steps to my own life I began to break down the "defined" and rigid God and venture inward to find the God I needed to do *my* work: strip the denial, peel away the layers, speak the truth and trust the outcome—to do the work. I encourage you to do the same.

Exercise:

1. Write what it will feel like for you to have a safe place to turn when you feel overwhelmed.

2. Write how you will experience this safe place (meditation, breathing, prayer, listening to music, taking a walk).

3. Write, in detail, how it feels to rely on this Source.

I recommend that you answer these questions from today's perspective and then answer them again as if they were already true. Some of you understand this and others are saying, "Huh? How can I write answers when I am not there?" We have a natural ability to daydream and fantasize, which is how some of the most successful people achieve their goals. They simply dream it, see it, write it down and keep it in their vision—they believe it can become a reality. If you don't believe you can get and stay organized, you won't. If you believe that you can but don't know how to do it, you are farther along than most, and the steps in this book will bring you the rest of the way—IF YOU DO THE WORK! You won't change anything or reach your goals without taking action, just as how you won't become thin without a diet and exercise program.

This step is fundamental to this program. It is the keystone to the rest, as without a strong foundation you may still make progress, but you will still feel like something is missing. It takes time to fully trust that you always have a safe place.

Within this strong foundation in progress, our remaining two principles for the first step begin to grab hold of us in our journey.

Hope: Elusive for some, for others hope was never within the realm of possibility. We felt so far down that it seemed a ridiculous idea. What's the point of hope, right? Have you been there? Have you felt so defeated, so depleted, that the idea of hope was laughable?

> HOPE: to expect with confidence; to cherish a desire *with anticipation*

Hope is the guiding light we can use. It's within us; it's our Source, our God. Hope helps allay the paralyzing fear that kept us from beginning this work in the first place, and it is a powerful tool that brings the rest of our life into the realm of possibility and that gives us permission to dream again— to dream aloud, to dream in color.

Finally, rounding out the principles is Faith. Faith carries hope when we forget that all things are possible with God. Faith reminds us of hope when we forget to dream. Faith shields hope from the people in our lives who disbelieve due to their own fear. Faith shields hope from the doubt-mongering echoes in our head that tell us how selfish we are for taking care of ourselves instead of them. Faith carries hope when we've uncovered yet another memory or feeling that makes us want to quit. Faith lifts hope up into view when we've lost sight of why we are doing the work we're doing. Faith is critical to the process.

> FAITH: Belief and trust in and loyalty to God (as you define Him/Her/It); firm belief in something for which there is no proof; complete trust

Keep faith simple; keep it all simple. After all, this is a very simple process. Just be cautious, however, not to confuse *simple* with *easy*. If it were easy there would be millions of people successfully recovered from the effects of clutter and disorganization. There's a very small percentage of people who would be willing to follow this simple program to get their desired result. It's not for those who need it; rather, it's for those who want it and are willing to do whatever it takes to have freedom and peace in their lives. Even if you've read this far into the book, you are FAR ahead of many.

I want to address the people who will appear and try to sabotage you as you do this work. It will be a challenge for you to NOT allow them to become your excuse to stop. Don't fall into that martyr role. Haven't you been there long enough? Really! Let's call that out right now. A martyr sacrifices themselves for the sake of others; they give to their own detriment. They think they are being of service, but when it appears they are unappreciated, as they often are, they become hurt, sad and resentful. This will be another one of the most difficult hurdles you'll face in this work. You will begin to unburden yourself of the "stuff" you've been carrying, you will become lighter, and the burdens of others will become clearer. You will realize that taking them on or allowing them in will seem heavier than usual. In other words, you'll experience others differently from before and you may wish to allow less of their interference in your life.

I know exactly what you are thinking: "I'm not going to abandon my family or friends in order to clear my clutter or do this work." Let me be clear that I'm not telling you to let go of anything or anyone; I'm simply telling you that, in my experience, when you begin to peel back the layers of clutter and denial and reveal the truth of an item or situation, you may feel differently about it. It would be detrimental for me to tell you to do anything of the sort. In fact, my intention is not to make you do anything; rather, I wish to give you the tools, the permission and the guidance to discover yourself and what really lies beneath the surface of clutter and disorganization. You get to move at a pace as fast or slow as your willingness and ability to be honest with yourself and others will allow. There is no timeline or deadline to this work. It's your life; you get to make the choices and call the shots. For some this is a completely new and foreign concept, so bring self-trust and faith back into your consciousness and continue reading.

As I said above, this DOES NOT mean that you are expected to release any relationships or change anything. In fact, I encourage you NOT to make any major decision concerning relationships for at least six months, maybe a year. Allow the principles and truths of this work to begin to settle in before you decide anything. With this work we often experience a profound change, a spiritual awakening, a heavy burden lifted and we become overzealous. We want to tell everyone who will listen to what we've learned. I encourage you to have a trusted friend to talk to and use your journal; be sure you have a safe place to funnel your emotions. Sharing them too soon with someone who doesn't understand what you're doing can be harmful to your process, and it could potentially be harmful to them, depending on their role in your journey.

To take care of yourself in the context of this step can come in many different forms. *Taking care* might mean physically taking care of yourself, e.g., getting help cleaning the kitchen to make sure you maintain a healthy environment, taking time out to cope with an onslaught of strong feelings, cleaning out a drawer or corner of your desk so you can feel you've made some progress, etc. You may need to have a Plan B thought out for when a loved one is not treating you with respect. This plan may call for a walk, a bath or a solitary drive, if you can do so safely. Removing yourself from an unsafe situation is not only your responsibility; it is your right. Did you take that in? You deserve to be safe, loved and respected!

I deserve to be safe, loved and respected by myself and others.

For some, this is another completely foreign concept. It is one of those messages rejected at the subconscious level because we cannot validate it to any message within ourselves that currently exists; the truth of that statement is buried so deeply inside ourselves that it seems impossible to hear—much less believe—at the intellectual level and more impossible to bring into the heart. This truth exists at the level where we know, and the idea that we are a precious human being in the eyes of God may be deeply buried. For some, this truth is entrenched in them because they never experienced it or had it validated by family growing up. As children, we become convinced it is not true if the people in our lives who are to love us unconditionally—our parents— mistreat, abuse or disregard us altogether. Chances are it didn't happen intentionally; they most likely did the best they knew to do. Our work in this book will be to hold that up to the light of the truth as well.

So how does this show up for us? We have received and invalidated; set out to prove that we are unsafe, unlovable and disrespectful all our lives; and we create situation after situation in our life to confirm it. Cracking it open and shining a light on it now causes it to recoil even farther inside of us, making this the reason this work isn't easy. Thus, we have to be willing to go against the grain that makes up the fabric of our internal message and change the whole pattern of our tapestry.

We are valuable human beings. We treat ourselves so badly because we believe—sometimes from a very early age—that we are worthless, stupid and unlovable. These messages may not have been directly verbalized, but through the behaviors of others, or possibly through the emotional unavailability of our parents, we may have internalized untruths and accepted their beliefs as our own.

We may have been physically, sexually or mentally abused as children or young adults, which from that we create a truth that if we shrink down or become invisible we won't get hurt. We create the truth that we need to preemptively hurt before we get hurt, that love hurts because someone hurt us and told us it's because they love us. Confusing? Yes. We create the truth that our value as human beings exists within our sexual function; that if we give ourselves sexually we'll be loved and we'll be enough. We create the truth that if we just work harder they'll love us when the truth is that we never really can do enough. We create the truth that if we say no we'll be left alone; if we stop doing for others they will be angry with us.

These truths aren't always the result of horrific situations. Sexual or physical abuse isn't the only thing that engenders these untruths. They come from all sorts of family dynamics, which are often bequeathed from generation to generation until someone takes the steps to break the cycle.

I want to welcome you to breaking the cycle of clutter and disorganization!

Step 1 Summary – Acknowledge

This is a momentous beginning to a shift in thinking and doing. Remember that this is a process, not a quick fix. You will work this and slowly see that your life is changing in many ways including how you feel about the clutter and how you value the clutter. It is important to acknowledge yourself and your progress no matter how big or small. This acknowledgement means you are becoming more aware of yourself and that you are moving ahead.

I hope you saw in this first step that it's critical to create a safe place for yourself—whether inside yourself or within your home—where you can have a place to regroup when things get heavy or overwhelming. In this space, you should be able to find God or Source; you should be able to curl up in the safety and strength of that power and rest your thoughts and body until you feel like you can move forward.

I hope you saw in this first step the cathartic value of writing your thoughts down and getting them out of your head, and I hope you will take the time to journal and share with someone that you love and that can be trusted to respect the sanctity of your journey.

I often remind my clients, "Remember, it often gets worse before it gets better." We don't like that because we always want to be moving forward. Don't allow yourself to believe that everything you do isn't making some sort of progress. You may not feel like you are blazing trails, but remember what I said earlier in the book, "Sometimes the greatest work is happening just below the surface."

Remember the affirmation from the beginning of this book and keep it posted for yourself around the house, office and car.

"I deserve to be safe, loved and respected by myself and others."

Step 2 – Investigate

The power and necessity of the first step becomes more apparent, which ushers us onto the next step. In the first step, we examined your willingness to do this work and the principles of honesty, hope and faith that must be put to practice. In this step, we are looking at courage and integrity.

In the first step, you established a plan so that you have a way to take care of yourself should you get overwhelmed. This will still come into play in this step, so when you get to a point where you find yourself stagnant or wish to give up, go back to the section where we discussed having a plan and look at what action you decided to take when this got overwhelming.

We knew it was likely, and it's okay. Use the plan to ensure you don't walk away from completing the process. You can no longer depend on others, luck, time or osmosis to get better; you must choose to move forward, driven by your own efforts. This is not to say you are alone. This just means that you must be the one to take action to move yourself toward the life you want to live. In fact, because you've created a safe relationship with someone to share with, they can play an important role for you in this step. They can be your objective source of grounding when you feel scared or overwhelmed. Being thorough is key, being willing to share is critical and having a trusted friend and a safe outlet are what make this effective.

In the previous step, we identified a power greater than ourselves that can guide us through this process. We must be willing to rely on that power to help us stay on course and keep from beating ourselves up when we fall back into old habits.

Let me be very clear: There is no perfect way to do this process. You will backslide, stumble, want to give up and get frustrated—OFTEN. After all, you're only human. If you have an impossible standard to try to keep to, you will not only fail, but you will beat yourself. Trust me: I have done this enough times to know that it's human nature to do that.

The power of this step is in the writing and sharing. Dedicating time to this activity, if even a few minutes a day, will determine whether or not you will succeed in moving forward. Remember when I talked about this being a simple, but not easy program? Well, here's where that statement rings true.

Remember when I talked about this program being available to everyone, but not everyone will apply it? Well, here's where that really shows up. This is the area of the work that challenges you.

The second step is really just about being willing to look at what's going on. If the space exists as the result of an event or lifestyle/behavior/belief, this step serves to explore that. It doesn't require monumental shifts, although they have been known to occur at this stage. Sometimes they simply come in shifts in perception that will forever change how you view a relationship or situation.

For me, this came about in a discussion with a trusted friend who was able to hold the mirror of truth up to me. She loved me enough to tell me the truth of my behavior. We were talking about my ideas of how someone had treated me badly and behaved inappropriately. A shift occurred for me in that conversation that allowed me to see that I had also behaved badly and that I had some responsibility in the dynamics of the relationship. This step allows us the opportunity to really scrutinize our lives today. Don't let that scare you, however, as the more you can embrace this part of the process, the more quickly you will find peace and serenity.

Do you know what I mean when I say that this is not an exercise to do from your head? Some of us have been living in our heads and figuring things out for so long that we don't know how to get back to the feelings. If you've been shut down to life, feelings or spirit, this step may take some time to produce results. It may be too painful to feel or look at this stuff. This is the place where it can feel like it is getting worse rather than getting better. It is only temporary as long as you continue to walk forward.

I want you to know that this is normal. If this were magic or easy, we would bypass the uncomfortable parts and—poof!—we'd be all better. However, it doesn't work like that. It takes time to allow the awareness to settle in before we even get to the place where we can begin to change our thinking and behavior. This work is the natural process, but the important piece is uncovering the areas that are keeping you stuck.

This isn't the place to analyze before writing answers down—this is the place to freely express yourself and allow all the truths to surface so that we can bring them forward for further examination. We tend to edit and judge with information based on our own experiences or we hold them up to unrealistic standards of ourselves or others. We think and feel things that we think no one else has ever thought or felt, and we make ourselves unique, which helps us continue to isolate ourselves.

When we think we are different from others it's easy to believe we are wrong, weird, unacceptable, etc. This feeds the shame and blame, especially if we isolate but try to make it someone else's fault for not welcoming us enough or correctly. We can use this as an excuse to shop or to stay alone in our stuff.

But...

So for those of you who are strong willed and have white-knuckled your way through life thus far, this section is for you. It's called BUT....

❑ But maybe I'll just *decide (AGAIN)* that I'll do it differently on my own.

❑ But why does this have to be so hard?

❑ But the clutter really is not that bad.

There is a power in putting pen to paper when journaling and writing out your feelings. I want to

I deserve to have a
fabulous,
clutter-free life!

emphasize the importance of putting pen to paper. Use your notebook or journal to do this work. Do not type it into your computer; it doesn't have the same effect. You may argue that you can write faster and more efficiently if you just type it into the computer. Okay, but DON'T. This isn't about getting it done faster or more efficiently; rather, this is actually about slowing down, feeling and processing as you write. If you type it in and buzz right through, you are missing the power of the exercise. I promise you may finish faster, but you won't get the long term results you desire if you type instead of write.

It would be ideal if you could choose a time to write that gives you the opportunity to devote your undivided attention. Though there is little quiet time in our busy lives, I encourage you to give yourself the gift of at least five minutes a day—even if that's all you can do—to write and to be with yourself. Write as much as you can. The more time you spend here in introspect, the better your results will be.

Before we begin the exercise, let's look at our principles for this section: courage and integrity. These are powerful words in the life of someone who has used clutter and disorganization as a replacement or supplement for courage and integrity.

This step involves looking into the space you continue to attempt to fill to see what is in there that is so insatiable. Without having created a foundation in the first step, it will be difficult to feel safe enough to really look as deeply as necessary to effectuate real change with this step.

> COURAGE: Mental or moral strength to venture, persevere and withstand danger, fear or difficulty.

I believe a key word in this definition is *persevere*. As adults, we do not have to be told what to do. We just need to be reminded and encouraged.

Integrity, as it is defined below, plays an important part in this process. Integrity grows and develops as you move your way through these steps.

> INTEGRITY: Firm adherence to a code of moral values; the quality or state of being complete or undivided; an unimpaired condition.

We may feel we are living our life with integrity. I mean, we're good people, right? As you work this program, you will learn a lot about yourself, and your perceptions and paradigms may shift and redefine themselves. What you once found acceptable or normal may become unacceptable.

For example, you may speak your mind without consideration for the feelings of others or the delivery of your message. Today you might find this gives you a sense of power, or you may not consider brash talk a problem. As you move through this process, you may find that you can effectively get your point across and, in fact, be better heard if you soften or change the way you communicate. It may be the slightest shift in self-awareness that creates a huge change in the quality of your relationships.

Shame & Blame

There are two great potential roadblocks to your success with this program, so let's look at them before they even get a chance to be an excuse for self-sabotage.

The first is shame, the painful feeling arising from the recognition of having done something dishonorable, improper or ridiculous. I believe those dealing with clutter and disorganization feel shame to be the number-one obstacle to reaching out for help. Shame, by its very definition is created by our own beliefs and self-judgment or the judgment of someone else that we allow to come into our energy. It is an overpowering force in our lives that has the ability to keep us isolated from friends, family and the world if we allow it to. Shame whispers into our ear at every opportunity in order to keep us from moving ahead, and while we may not directly or consciously label it shame, that's what it is.

Shame keeps us looking down rather than ahead; it allows others to walk over us rather than see us. Shame keeps the truth a secret and convinces us that it's not okay to share it. Blame keeps the focus on others. Shame and blame partner together to keep us stuck in the problem. They dance together to keep the cycle going; they tag team to keep you stuck.

Shame keeps the secrets. All those things you know and feel that you think are the deepest, darkest, never-gonna-tell-anyone kinds of things. Do you have some of those? Underneath the shame is the truth of who we are, our purest spiritual belief and experience. The truth is waiting patiently to be released, but the weight and depth of shame has buried it so deeply.

Because we are spiritual beings having a human experience, we live our lives on life's path. Regardless of your religious upbringing, whether very devout or none at all, it's important to be willing to open your mind to new ideas.

It has been my experience that clutter and disorganization are symptomatic behaviors that need to be realized in order for the problems caused by clutter and disorganization to disappear. When we discontinue the behavior, we are left with the problems that CAUSED the behavior. These are what we begin to uncover in the questions below. These are the things that created the void we so diligently try to fill with stuff.

If you find that a particular question stirs painful or distressing memories, write it down, even if it doesn't seem to answer the question or make sense. This is a safe place to release those thoughts and ideas so you can further examine how they have played a part in your life until now. If you start to self-edit as you are writing, allow that to come out and be written too! I promise you that the more you allow yourself to be free and honest, the better your results will be. We have been bound by our secrets, and even if you decide this is not safe to share with someone else, much of the power has been taken out of it by putting it on paper. It is not important for it to be logical, neat or in any specific format, the writing often takes on a life of its own when we allow the process to happen.

I have experienced this on many occasions, primarily in working through this process on my own but also through journaling with my left hand. I am a right-handed person but have done exercises where I have used my right hand to ask a question and allowed my spirit or inner child to answer through my left. When using this very free flowing means of expression, some startling answers were revealed to me about the abuse of my childhood. I was able to come to some great levels of acceptance about those people who played a part in that abuse, and I have been able to forgive based on the truth that was written. Writing and allowing the truth to come through the pen to paper is incredibly powerful. The tip of the pen is much like the narrow end of a funnel, it takes all that feels big and overwhelming and directs it into a manageable size to get it exactly where it needs to go. Visualize your thoughts flowing through a funnel of truth out onto the paper.

Shifting gears back to the questions: I am not promoting regression work here; I am asking you to glance back at what experiences you have had in life and how they affect your behavior today. At birth, we are exposed to our parents' behaviors, beliefs, expectations and attitudes, which came from their parents and so on. The purpose of this exercise is not to go back and find who to blame. We already determined that blame keeps us from the work we are trying to do because it keeps us focused outside ourselves although the solution is inside. We are going forward to change what we can.

Pay attention to your reaction to some of these questions, especially if you have a strong response or refusal to answer. It is in these times that I'm asking you to look even more intently at the answer. You may react strongly to a question that stirs discomfort or asks you to look at something you don't want to look at.

Finally, once again, there is no perfect time and place to begin this work. Trust me when I say that there will always be a dish to do, a bed to make, trash to take out, a call to make or any other possible distraction you can come up with to avoid the work. I know. I've used them all. Even as I write this paragraph, I had to bring myself back from distractions to write. When you notice it happening, acknowledge it and do your best to get back on task. One way to do that is by using a timer and giving yourself 5 minutes to start. I often hear of people who spend so much time getting ready to write that they run out of time to write. Just begin and do what you can each time you do it. Don't fool yourself into thinking there is a legitimate reason you can't begin. Until now, it's been all about excuses, so why wouldn't you pull out all the stops to NOT sit down and do the work? Be aware that this is going to happen and that it's normal.

Questions for investigating the space:

- Have you ever been organized? If yes, write about when the shift to disorganization happened for you.

- Was there an action or event that you remember that changed how you handle life? Describe the feelings around that shift. Were you rebelling, defeated?

- What kind of relationship did your mother have with her parents?

- What kind of relationship did your father have with his parents?

- Write about your family dynamics. Where are you in the birth order? What was your family's financial situation? How was conflict handled? Was there laughter?

- Did you have a hard time pleasing one or both of your parents?

- Did your family move often? If so, did you make friends and then have to let them go? How did you deal with that?

- Did you have chores as a child? What were they? Did you resent having to do them?

- Was there structure and discipline in your home growing up?

- Write about your best and worst childhood memories. Why these memories?

❧ Were you treated as a nuisance or a burden?

❧ Did you experience sexual abuse as a child? Write about that.

❧ Did you have feelings of worthlessness?

❧ Write about your friendships. What kind of friend were you?

❧ Were you a troublemaker? Did you defy authority? Did you get into fights?

❧ Were you a peacemaker? Did you sacrifice yourself or your beliefs to keep the peace?

❧ Did anything happen in high school that was a continuing source of shame? Did you feel deep down that you lacked an identity of your own?

❧ What was the most embarrassing incident of adolescence? Are there any others that you remember?

❧ Were you jealous or envious of others?

❧ Did you give the spiritual side of life consideration? Did you choose to believe that your human intelligence is the last word?

❧ Are you afraid of getting too close to another person for fear of being rejected?

- Do you test your relationships repeatedly, looking for slights or any differences in order to find some grounds for complaint?

- Define *Love*. What do you feel it is? Do you drift in and out of relationships? Does it seem that people mean little to you?

- Why did you get married? Or, why haven't you gotten married? Was the marriage for the right reasons? Do you share in the responsibilities for the family's problems?

- Does diversion and distraction interfere with your adult goals? Do you believe that your situation is not really hopeless and that you are capable of improving it?

- What is your greatest fear?

- Do you have a pattern of getting sick? Do you use illness as an excuse to avoid responsibilities or to get attention or sympathy?

- Are your expectations unreasonable?

- How do you think it would be different if "they" were out of your life?

- Are you uncomfortable in social situations?

🍂 Have you been so busy making money that your family sees little of you?

🍂 Are you able to be yourself and be honest with others about who you are?

🍂 Do you have difficulty arriving places on time?

🍂 This step is an opportunity to look a little deeper and ask ourselves if there is a payoff in the chaos. Is there something that we gain by running behind? Do we somehow find comfort in being a victim of our clutter?

Step 2 Summary – Investigate

We have begun the process of investigating your perceptions and feelings about the experiences in your life up till now. The intention behind the questions is to create some insight into what's working and what's not working in your life and why you show up the way you do. As I said before, when we write this stuff down and share it with someone else it alleviates the discomfort of its secrecy. Start thinking about a trusted friend that you might be willing to share your writing with. By acknowledging it and investigating it, we can now look at how to shift your perceptions and behavior around it so that you can live the life you dream of living.

This is the place in the process where we connect experiences to the value we put on the physical clutter in our homes, we also look at how clutter is serving us. Does it serve to keep you isolated? Does it keep you overwhelmed so you don't have to feel the feelings that the questions address? This is an important place to contemplate the clutter and disorganization in your life.

Step 3 - Release

You did a great job answering the questions in the previous section. I hope you learned a lot about yourself. What's amazing about this process is that you may choose to go back and answer those again at a later time and come up with more details and sometimes different answers. This is the evidence that this is not a one-shot quick fix; it's a process.

With all that you have learned about yourself and your life to this point, we begin the process of releasing the things that keep us stuck, habits that are no longer effective, old ways of thinking that no longer serve and even grudges or resentments toward others that serve no other purpose than to punish them and ultimately keep us stuck.

We've come to a place where our pride often causes us to become stuck between peaceful freedom and holding on to old beliefs and the power we think we have by being right. You may have heard it before: "Would you rather be right or happy?"

This is where you may have to push yourself out of your comfort zone a bit. You may be choosing to read this book through one time before doing the actual work. I hope you choose to go back and do the exercises, put up the sticky notes and allow yourself the time to do the work. These next sections will make a lot more sense and you'll get real results if you will invest in yourself. If you choose not to, you can always remember, "If nothing changes, nothing changes."

If nothing changes, nothing changes.

You may find, from time to time, that during this process you feel you have done nothing and that you might as well quit now. Why dredge up more stuff? You may also want to know how long it will take or how you will know if you're doing a good job. When I talk with my organizing clients, we often discuss that it may seem like it is getting worse when, in fact, you sometimes have to dishevel things a bit before you can get them back in the right order. The same is true for this process, but instead of your things getting messed up, it may be your perceptions and emotions. This is where it's critical to have a friend to encourage you and a connection with Source that allows you to silence your worries and hear that ever-so-small voice telling you you're okay.

> You are challenging
> realities that have been in
> place for your whole life; you
> can expect that there will be
> some resistance to change.
> - Kelli Wilson

You'll know you're doing it if you're uncomfortable but still willing to continue. Put this on a yellow sticky note to remind you on the challenging days.

> "And the day came when
> the risk to remain tight in a
> bud was more painful than
> the risk it took to blossom."
> - Anais Nin

I've talked about willingness throughout the book—willingness to trust God and the process, willingness to risk and willingness to put yourself first—but it really plays a large role in this section. Willingness does not mean that you have to like it; rather, it means that you choose to remain open to the possibilities and take action anyway. Unlike the definition below, you may have dealt with a great deal of reluctance but were able to complete the work anyway. If so, great job.

> Willingness: Accepted by
> choice or without reluctance;
> prompted to act or respond

As we begin to better understand ourselves and our behavior, we can see patterns more clearly. With clarity comes humility; with humility comes freedom.

You may see that you experienced a great deal of loss—whether an isolated event or a series of them—in your life, but you minimized its effects. You may have discovered in Step 2 that you weren't allowed to talk about loss or perhaps those around you acted as if it didn't happen. Perhaps your grief was never honored or permitted.

In this case, there are many potential dynamics materializing. There's loss that precipitates grief, which based on what we learned from Craig Nakken, activates a cycle of grief and healing. Perhaps the loss was minimized or denied, which often opens the void. Unless we take the time to work through and deal with the emotions, we will likely end up trying other things to keep the feelings down or numb ourselves to them. This is the purpose shopping, clutter and chaos serve.

When we acknowledge and look at what happened—I mean really look at it and allow ourselves to feel it—the healing can begin. A difficult but important part in this process is the willingness to see what part you played in the situation. Think about whether you created it or stirred it up and kept it going, either internally or externally.

Stirring it up and keeping it going internally means obsessively thinking about it or wondering, "What if I had done it differently?"

Stirring it up and keeping it going externally means talking it over and over with others. Taking the same story to many different people in order to try to soothe yourself or justify your story—to be right.

Regardless of how you keep it going, the fact is that you keep it going. The truth is that you did the best you could at the time. This is where you choose to make this a learning experience and move forward into making different choices in the future.

You probably know humiliation all too well – but humility may be new.

> HUMILITY: the quality or state of being humble
>
> HUMBLE: not proud or haughty, not arrogant or assertive, reflecting, expressing or offered in a spirit of submission

In this definition, I want to examine the word *reflecting*. Here I believe it is a precursor to *humble*, but I see it differently. In my experience, reflecting is a key requisite of humility. Until we look at ourselves, reflect, we cannot attain humility. If we continue to view the world as if we were on the receiving end of its will rather than how we are participants in the collective experience, we will feel victimized and defensive. Humility cannot exist in either of these roles.

Earlier I said that with clarity comes humility, and with humility comes freedom. There are times when clarity and humility are interchanged; you may have a moment of clarity about a possession, a person or your behavior, which creates that eureka moment where you see yourself more clearly than ever before. Have you experienced this? Sometimes in these humbling moments we can unchain ourselves from those old paradigms and see ourselves in a new way such as, for example, vulnerable, stubborn or wrong. Humility, in turn, permits clarity. You may have a moment when you experience a vulnerable moment with a loved one or while alone, and for the first time, you see yourself in a different way. See how it works?

The questions are meant to help provoke these kinds of awarenesses because it's with the awareness that begins the change. Much like the onion metaphor we often hear when talking about our journey in life, there are many layers that will be peeled back throughout this process if you continue to do the work.

This step is important for a several reasons:

1. It helps to begin separating the truth from the lies. This is necessary because until now you have made decisions about your life based on your current reality. You wouldn't be reading this book if you were fully satisfied with how that's working for you, so you get to redefine what is true for you and about you.

2. It helps to begin taking the power out of guilt, shame and blame. This is critical if you are to live a life of peace and serenity. Guilt, shame and blame take up a lot of mental, physical and spiritual energy. It's impossible to have a peaceful life

when you are full of guilt and shame or spending lots of energy trying to blame someone else for the condition of your life.

3. It creates a slower pace of life. When you are burdened by secrets, you must often keep yourself busy in a variety of ways to avoid quiet moments where your painful truths can bubble up and try to surface. Many times fast-paced, quickly speaking people who won't listen to what others have to say are working hard to keep from feeling.

4. It will bridge the gap between your head and your heart. Many of us have experienced such pain that we avoid being present in our bodies. We live our lives from an intellectual standpoint, never really experiencing life from the heart as a spiritual being. Much like the benefit described above, this step will help remove much of the pain that keeps us from fully integrating our head with our heart, a distance that I often share is a million miles apart. It takes work, but it's worth it.

You may have had some astonishing awarenesses while answering the questions. Another part of this step is sharing that information with a trusted friend. We'll talk about how that works, but before we do, I want to share with you why it's important.

Our minds are very powerful and persuasive. When we are threatened, we react with the thought or action that is most ingrained in us—our instincts, if you will. I mentioned earlier that we are living the best life possible based on our current reality, and many of us are living very intellectually. Our minds have created a reality that keeps us 'safe,' so any threat to that safety or any challenge to our reality will summon our survival mode, causing us to revert back to familiar behavior. For many people, their life works just fine living this way, and they feel no urge to challenge their beliefs or investigate the need for change. They may not be open to exploring a different possibility, as they are fine with their life as it is. However, isn't the reason you picked up this book because clutter and disorganization have taken over your life and you want different results? Well then, we have to address this powerful mind and the messages it tells us when we try to feed it new information.

A majority of our decisions concerning how we live our life is based on information that comes from our unconscious and our subconscious mind. Thirty percent of our actions and thoughts are based on what our unconscious mind holds—those repressed thoughts and experiences—60 percent of our actions and thoughts come from our subconscious mind and only 10 percent comes from conscious thought. This step focuses on that 60 percent: the subconscious mind. The subconscious mind holds the truths of us and our world and is the mechanism that rebuffs when you try to introduce a new truth. For example, you may choose to put up the yellow sticky from Step 1—I deserve to be safe, loved and respected by myself and others—and you may have resisted doing so because you do not believe it is true. However, you are willing to take a risk and trust this process, so you post it anyway. You may read it each day, maybe several times a day, as you go about your business. Each time you read it aloud or in your head it gets less and less uncomfortable, and sometimes quickly, sometimes slowly, you begin to believe it. After a while, you find yourself in a situation where you get to practice being safe by leaving a situation where you are not being respected or you feel your physical or emotional safety has been jeopardized. You're amazed. The action of telling yourself a different truth turned into acting differently. Acting in this new way will reprogram the subconscious so that the next time you are presented with a situation that is unsafe or not respectful you will find that you make the new choice without much thought. This doesn't mean that you won't revert back to old behavior, but when you do you will recognize it far more quickly and you will be able to get yourself back on track.

I experienced this firsthand. It's funny how we react when we realize we are doing things differently. I was ending a particularly toxic relationship where our communication was awful. We didn't know how to hear or be heard, we didn't know how to say what we meant without being mean and we were not nice to each other at all. During these conversations, I would often find myself paralyzed on one end of the phone listening to some pretty disturbing things being said to me. I knew I didn't want to hear it, but it never dawned on me that I didn't deserve it—that it was unsafe and disrespectful. It wasn't until I shared it with someone else who had experienced it that they suggested I could hang up the phone, telling me I didn't deserve that treatment. The idea was foreign. Wouldn't that just make it worse later? I remember the first time I mustered up the courage to hang up the phone. I mean, I listened and thought about hanging up for a while, and then with ALL I had in me at the time, I closed my cell phone and put it down. "Oh my goodness, what have I done?" Well, I had taken care of myself. Now, if I find myself in that situation with a loved one or ANYONE for that matter, I simply hang up the phone. Some of you may be thinking, "Duh! Hang up the phone." But imagine any other scenario where YOU are or have been frozen and had considered doing something differently but were paralyzed.

Another note on this story is that it took me more time to learn not to pick up the phone when the person called right back to continue the argument. I can look back with humor at this behavior now, but the key message here is that IT IS A PROCESS!

Ready to work?

Take out your notebook and write about three to five of these areas where you wish to take a different action. Without thinking about the consequences of your actions, write how you would like to do it differently. I tell you not to think about the consequences yet because I want you to write what you would do from a place of power and safety. Don't get too far ahead into what might happen if you say this or do that right now. Just envision yourself full of courage and write out the scenario, like my real life example above.

Maybe for you it's replying to the voice in your own head that says "Keep it" with a new phrase: "I don't need it" or "Is this serving my life for the best?" Perhaps you have a loved one who says things that makes you feel bad or guilty about keeping things, or perhaps they guilt you into keeping things. Maybe you would love to tell them that you are doing the best you can or that you are going to donate a particular item to charity. Or perhaps you feel like this person does not listen or they do not respect your wishes. Maybe you would like to say, "Thank you, but I do not want to do that right now."

I encourage you to write these scenarios down to get them on paper so that you can be clear. Don't forget the power of putting pen to paper: It tends to take away the confusion when we stop it from spinning around inside our head. Once you write them down you can keep them in a safe place and read them aloud to yourself or in the mirror. This is the practicing part we talked about where we are to choose different behaviors. Here you will begin to feel a shift in how you feel when you say it. That doesn't mean it won't be frightening to act differently with someone by saying how we feel or by behaving differently; rather, it will be empowering, regardless of how they take it. It is important that you know that this may take you days, weeks or months of practicing to yourself before you feel you can say it to someone else. Even more importantly, you must know that it doesn't matter how long it takes. It's *your* experience and *your* journey. Don't let anyone impose time constraints on your life lessons.

When you are ready to step into speaking the truth, it's important to remember the phrase below that we learned earlier in the book from the section called "A little more about the space."

What someone else thinks of me is none of my business

> Our biggest fear is not in expressing the truth but that we will be attacked or belittled because of our truth.
> – Kelli Wilson

Our biggest fear is not in expressing the truth but that we will be attacked or belittled because of our truth. Sometimes this is a valid fear, and sometimes we have created a scenario in our head based on truths from our past that we have continued to feed. This is where the continued work of discovering these truths that rule us and debunking them with reality becomes so important. In this critical step, you must continue to look within at your reality, to hold it up to the light of life today and determine whether it is still valid and whether it serves you well or inhibits you from living a fuller life.

Back in my story about hanging up the phone during the fight, it wasn't as much about hanging up as it was about my fear that this person would abandon *me* rather than *me* leaving him. My fear was about conflict. See, if I stayed on the phone and internalized the abuse without saying anything, I felt like I was a victim. I thought that if I took action and hung up I would trigger more conflict. We teach people how to treat us and I had allowed this behavior for a long time. Empowering myself and taking responsibility was daunting because it also meant that I had to look at my part in the behavior. I ultimately had to look at why I showed up for abuse, why I chose people who would treat me like that and what part I had in creating the drama. Remember "stirring the drama" from the beginning of this section? Well, I realized I needed to create the drama so that I could be the victim—the martyr.

Here are some questions to contemplate and write about:

- How are you showing up as a victim in your relationship with clutter?

- How are you showing up as a victim in your relationship with people?

- How are you showing up as a martyr in your relationship with clutter?

- How are you showing up as a martyr in your relationship with people?

- What are you afraid will happen if you tell the truth or go against the grain?

- What is the truth about your fear?

I mentioned earlier that it is important in this step to have a trustworthy friend with whom to talk about the changes you are experiencing, someone who can listen without judging or telling you what you do. Sharing their experience with you is great as long as they are sharing with you and not telling you what to do. You may choose a friend to share some of these things with, but you may also choose a professional for some of the deeper realizations. A therapist, minister or counselor is better equipped to handle situations where you may have become aware of some abuse or other heavier experiences. This book is not meant to counsel you, but some of the questions and processes may create an opportunity for your mind and body to reveal things that help with your spiritual growth. Just remember, our bodies, our spirit, our higher power is working for our greater good and would not reveal to you something you are not equipped to handle. I encourage you to seek help on issues that feel like more than your journal and trusted friend can handle.

The actions of this step include answering questions and writing about specific areas in your life in which you wish to show up differently. It's also important in this step to share what you are learning with someone else. Our spiritual growth, our healing, does not happen when we try to do it all alone. It just doesn't work that way. We can read volumes about healing ourselves and make progress, but I feel that true healing is done with others.

So I'm sure you can see even more clearly now, by your work in this step, that this book is about way more than just clutter. In this step, Step 3, we will further examine the patterns and other areas needing attention uncovered through your work in Step 2. I hope you are continuing to embrace the truth about the stuff and that you can see how slight, persistent effort on your part can change how you see your life and how you see your clutter.

There is another action to take in this step, and it's an action directly between you and your God, whatever name you have chosen to call that power greater than you to work with and to guide you through this process. This additional action is where you begin to create a stronger connection between you and Source so that you can really use what you have learned so far to continue to grow, trust and see results from this work.

Throughout this book, I have talked about having a power greater than you to turn to, to depend on and to trust to guide you through the experiences you are to have. I realize that many people may continue to be challenged with the concept of something bigger than they are—something that is always working *for* you and never against you. I'm not here to convince anyone that they should choose a certain religion or believe a certain way, but I am here to encourage you to believe that the universe is working in your favor: sometimes in the form of delivering wonderful people and things into our lives, sometimes in the form of presenting the truth (how we judge it is up to us), sometimes in presenting us the opportunity to learn a lesson and grow and sometimes to create in our lives abundance beyond our wildest dreams.

I believe this idea that the universe, our higher power, is working for us and never against us is fundamental. For me, I know that this has been an intuitive truth for me all my life, but the events of my life—my abuse, divorce, financial insecurities—have contradicted that. So I thought. Through my own work on these steps I realized that the more I cleared out the wreckage of my life and looked at those experiences as opportunities, the better I felt about what I could allow into my life. I believe it's all out there in queue waiting for us to allow it; it's our beliefs that keep it from coming in. I didn't conjure up this idea: It's the universal law of attraction. What we believe and focus on grows, and we attract what we believe.

This next activity, when practiced, will help break the outdated habits and behaviors you are trying to change and replace them with useful and helpful actions. It builds on the work you have already done in this section and will continue the momentum every time you peel back another layer. Keep exploring more and more the areas you wish to change and the questions while applying this activity.

Any change we wish to make takes effort to begin the shift. I've learned from experience that you cannot force a solution without (negative) results, whether immediately or sometime down the road. The most productive yet challenging thing to do is trust the process and let the solution come in its divine time. This is contrary to the way we were raised, and it's contrary to our determination to figure it out on our own. The truth is that if we lay the groundwork, do the footwork (homework) and trust that what we need will come, what we need will come.

A daily affirmation is the next action. I'm going to give you a few examples that you can use to get started, but you will ultimately have to create your own based on your beliefs and desires so as to craft a moving, living verse that will be one of your *greatest* tools in this program. This is when you spur the flow of positive energy into your life, your consciousness and your spiritual awareness. In this step, you will begin to intuitively handle situations that used to trip you up and fluster you, and you will start seeing yourself and others differently. This is where the shift in perspective and perception will change everything you wish to be— and allow to be—changed. The action is to choose and read an affirmation each day, preferably frequently, and allow the possibilities.

Affirmations:
(substitute your name for God
throughout the affirmation)

1. God, I accept good and peaceful times into my life now. Please remove those beliefs that no longer serve me and that no longer serve you. I am free from concern about _____ and am so grateful for _____. Show me the truth you wish me to see. (fill in the blanks)

2. God, I pray that you remove the challenges preventing me from allowing joy and abundance in my life. Show me how to help myself and others. Please reveal to me what you want me to know and see so that I can be the person you want me to be.

3. Source, thank you for removing from me those beliefs that no longer serve me. Thank you for moving me through my clutter and

disorganization. I am grateful for the calm, abundant and full life I am living today.

Step 3 Summary ~ Release

We did a lot of work in this step by shedding the beliefs and truths that no longer serve us in our pursuit of the best life possible. Hopefully you can see that clutter and disorganization have only been the symptoms for the clutter inside yourself. I encourage you to continue reviewing and reworking this step so that you can uncover more and more opportunities to move toward the life you want to live.

In the next section we will look at how to keep this going.

Step 4 – Maintain

I want to encourage you to recognize yourself for all the work you have done in Steps 2 and 3. Founded on Step 1, those really are the action steps of the whole program, and I encourage you to rework them in order to keep the process going. I guarantee you that, each time you go through them, you will discover more about yourself—if not new information, at least a better or different understanding of who you are. Keep peeling the onion!

You have done a lot of work and it's important to keep the momentum going by creating some ways to really root the new thinking and behavior into your everyday life. The intention is to make these new ideas, these truths that you have uncovered, the norm for how you live your life going forward. The goal is to make them the instinct that you default to when you get knocked off track or face a challenge.

When we make a foundational change in ourselves, the greatest challenge we face is in trusting the results, incorporating them into every day and sustaining that change. You know because you've been there before. You've worked really hard to get caught up in an area of your life—get ahead of the clutter, lose a few pounds, change an attitude toward someone or something—only to have it fade away and revert to the way it was, right?

This step is all about the perseverance that is needed to create and maintain the life you want to live. Perseverance is at the foundation of keeping anything going and the spirituality is maintaining and nurturing the connection you developed with God or whatever it is you choose to call that power greater than yourself. Let's look at the definitions of these words before we get into the actions of this step.

> Perseverance: Steady persistence in a course of action, a purpose, a state, etc., especially in spite of difficulties, obstacles or discouragement

I love this definition particularly because it includes the "especially in spite of difficulty" aspect. We can all persevere when the going is good, but when we feel overwhelmed, stuck or defeated and we push through anyway, that's what truly defines *perseverance* and it makes the end results even more gratifying.

I have practiced martial arts for many years. Each session concludes with the recital of this affirmation, "As a dedicated student of the martial arts, I will live by the principles of black belt: modesty, courtesy, integrity, perseverance, courage and indomitable spirit." Perseverance is key in martial arts and in life. You can become a dedicated student of your organizing goals and continue the work—physically and spiritually—in order to reach the goals you have set for yourself.

Our instructor frequently reminded us of a few other sayings I want to share with you: "Never, never, never, never give up" and "Fall seven times; rise eight. Life begins from here." These have become mantras for me and are tools I regularly use when I feel defeated or overwhelmed. I encourage you to make one or all of these a yellow sticky note so you remember that YOU CAN DO IT. It's the reminder that slight, persistent effort can move you successfully forward in *anything* you do. But never forget that it's a process and that it will take time before it becomes natural for you. I remember the first time I stepped onto the mat at the martial arts school. I was uncoordinated and confused and had to be reminded that it took lots of time and practice for those instructors and students ahead of me to get to where they were. It was a process for them much like this is a process for you.

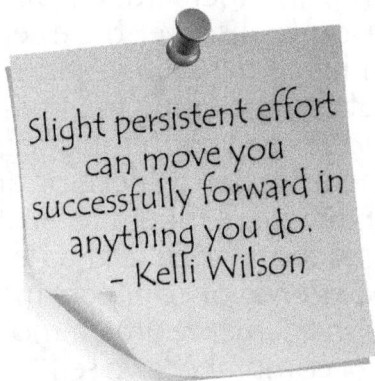

Slight persistent effort can move you successfully forward in anything you do.
– Kelli Wilson

Let's define *spirituality* and talk more about how to work this into daily care and maintenance. It's not a simple definition, as its interpretation is largely arbitrary, so I'll give you the technical definition, a Wikipedia definition and my opinion. I encourage you to take some time to think about what it means to you.

SPIRITUAL: the quality or fact of being spiritual, predominantly spiritual character as shown in thought, life, etc.; spiritual tendency or tone.

Wikipedia definition of Spirituality: Spirituality can refer to an ultimate reality or transcendent dimension of the world; an inner path enabling a person to discover the essence of his or her being. Spiritual practices, including meditation, prayer and contemplation, are intended to develop an individual's inner life. Such practices often lead to an experience of connectedness with a larger reality, a more comprehensive self.

Become a student of yourself, fearless in your pursuit to uncover as much as possible. You will be amazed at the change in your life if you employ the steps and principles of this program. I hope you'll write to share it with me. I can't wait to hear about it!

It is important to create a closer relationship with your Higher Power, which is the spiritual principle of this step. Spiritual maintenance as your priority will create astonishing shifts in all other facets of your life. Trust me on this one; I'm living proof. I can tell you on any given day that my ability to communicate, be patient, to trust, to be productive and so much more are direct results of my spiritual wellbeing. When I am not taking care of myself and connecting with God, I am less of the person I want to be and more of the person I used to be.

We discussed in the beginning of this book, and I want to reiterate, that *spiritual* in the context of the work we're doing here is NOT the same as religion. In my opinion, spirituality is a state of being, regardless of and including your religious practice, where you are connected to a Power greater than yourself on a regular basis and open to the guidance and teachings that come from this Power. It's the willingness to accept that life events are intended for the growth of one's soul during its human experience.

There is much that can be said in regards to spiritual growth. The action of this step is to explore your own spiritual growth through the context of this book with your trusted friend and through the connection with your Higher Power. There are many ways to do this. Your action in this step is to begin an activity as a way to maintain a daily connection with your Higher Power so that you can continue to grow spiritually. This daily connection is what allows you to continue to be open to learning and exploring yourself, and it keeps you in the moment and in your own business rather than focusing everywhere else except on yourself.

If you are willing to learn and explore yourself, you will find that the more you clean out your spiritual space, the easier it will be to clean out your physical space: your home and life. This is the magic of the program. The more you do to uncover and resolve what has kept you spiritually, mentally and physically stuck, the more unrestrained you will become to move ahead. It works, and it takes time and perseverance to be willing to learn more about yourself, but it's worth it!

If you're willing to be in the moment, you'll be amazed at how your life will change. Fear and overwhelm do not exist in the moment; rather, they surface when we're thinking about the past or future. When we are in the moment, doing what is right in front of us we can be calm. Think about that...

If you're willing to take care of yourself and mind your own business, you'll be amazed at the amount of time you have available to do the work of this book. You'll be amazed at the progress you can make, as well as how light and free your life will feel.

You are worth the work! I hope you'll commit to daily activity to move yourself in the direction of serenity and freedom in life. Choose the activity that works best for you based on what you know about yourself, what you're willing to do and even what time of day you will be at your best to do it.

Up ahead are some ideas for this activity. I encourage you to try them to see which of them is a good fit for you.

We are all at different stages of spiritual maintenance. I want you to know that you should not expect to just sit down and begin meditating an hour a day. It takes some people years to get to a place where they can do that. Some days we may fall out of bed and say, "God, please help me." I want you to know that these two examples and *everything* in between are okay. It takes time to find what's going to work for *you*, and even then it takes time to start practicing it regularly. You may have to set an appointment with yourself for 5 minutes of quiet time. This is okay too.

Spiritual Maintenance

❑ Sit quietly, say "Thank you and please direct me today."

❑ Write a list of things for which you are grateful.

❑ At the end of the day, write down 3 things that you recognize as personal growth and say, "Thank you, I am willing to learn."

❑ Each day read a piece of inspirational literature that inspires you and makes you smile.

❑ Read the list of things for which you are grateful.

❑ Call a friend and ask them how they are doing. Don't talk about you; just listen. (Sometimes our Higher Power talks to us through friends.)

❑ Attend your church or other group activity. Smile at people there.

❑ Sit quietly and ask, "What will you have me do today, God?" Listen for the answer.

Step 4 Summary - Maintain

We've done a lot of work and you are moving confidently in the direction of maintaining the efforts. Remember that it won't be perfect. You are human and you will have days when it's just not possible to sit quietly and connect with your Higher Power. On these days it's okay to give yourself permission to be human and know that as soon as you can you will take the time to connect and take care of yourself. You'll find that, as time goes on and you continue to practice these steps and principles, it will take less and less effort to stay on track, and you'll recognize when you feel off track a lot sooner than ever before. This daily practice and the work prior will begin to set the foundation for expanding into your physical environment where the clutter may still be looming over you. Know that your external environment is a reflection of your internal environment, once you feel you are moving forward on the inside job you'll be much better equipped for the physical clutter

Do you feel like you have done incredible work? How will you celebrate yourself and your efforts? I encourage you to do something nice for yourself, whether it's a physical self care like a massage or manicure, or maybe it's a movie or lunch out. Do something to acknowledge that you are taking exceptional care of you.

Step 5 – Share

In the previous steps we discovered how we had to learn to allow for self-care and put ourselves first—very foreign concepts to many of us. Much of this process has been about just that: learning about ourselves, looking within ourselves and taking care of ourselves first. This idea is much like the cliché story about being in an airplane and putting your mask on first before assisting others. It's a challenging concept and one worth repeating because many of us are where we are in our life and clutter because we don't take care of ourselves.

I remember hearing this airplane analogy many years before I began my own work. I truly believed that I was taking care of myself. I mean, I got up every day, brushed my teeth and showered; I ate when I was hungry. Isn't that what it means to take care of myself? My own limited thinking and self-awareness led me to believe that was so.

Later I learned that taking care of my physical self was fundamental to being human. Hey, some people struggle with even the basics. I began to realize that taking care of myself was not only physical, but mental and spiritual as well. Mentally, I needed to feed myself with knowledge and information that expanded my mind in a positive way (I had been battling negative thoughts and perceptions all my life). This meant that I had to begin to look at who I was spending time with and what kind of information we were sharing: Were we self-deprecating, gossiping or bashing the character of loved ones or strangers? What you focus on grows, so if a majority of your time and energy is focused on negative thoughts and behaviors, it makes sense that much of your life's results reflect that. If I choose to focus on the good or opportunity in a situation, I will begin to see positive results.

Taking care of my spiritual self meant I had to take inventory of the resentments I harbored toward others, as these resentments are self-defeating and they damage us to a far greater extent than the other person in most cases. When the venom of resentment fills us and manifests in our attitude toward the individual, it seeps into other relationships as well. Its effects are powerful, but we don't always realize it.

For example: A wife resents her husband, and eventually, their relationship deteriorates to divorce. Her resentment continues to be directed at him, but when he is not around, it manifests in anger or frustration at the kids, family or strangers. Extended family who support the husband also fall victim to her ill feelings because of their support. It can go on from there to reach many others who don't deserve it.

This is my story: As I began my spiritual journey and relinquished my resentments toward others, it freed me up to begin caring for myself. When my needs are met I can begin to think of others and be of service to them. In this step, this means sharing with others and helping to encourage their growth. I caution you to remember this critical factor about giving back and doing for others: You must only serve from where you overflow, which means taking care of your needs above the needs of others. If you fall back into martyrdom, resentment will be close behind. I know, I know, I can hear the "say what?" already. This is a simple concept, but we make it complicated with our need to be a victim or a martyr. It can be confusing as a mom, especially, because we sometimes give up everything for our kids. Think about how much you can give your family and your children when you are happy, healthy and spiritually inspired.

When it comes to nurturing and caring for others, you need to have experienced it to be truly effective at helping someone else experience it. The principle for this step is service.

> SERVICE: An act of helpful activity; help; aid; to do someone a service

You can find many ways to serve from your overflow. Sometimes it's as simple as an encouraging word or a word of empathy so that another person knows they are not alone.

❑ Perhaps you share with others in a small group at church or school

❑ Maybe you suggest this book to a friend

❑ Maybe you tell someone your story so they do not feel like they are the only one

If your own work is being done, you will know where you can be of service. At that point, the universe, God, Source, will present you with myriad opportunities to give back! Trust me, I know.

I'm sure by now you can understand, unlike many, how liberating it is to clear the spiritual, mental and physical clutter with a more lasting effect. You have been changed. This final step in the clutter healing process is critical: In order to keep what you have you must give it away. This is one of many paradoxes in the spiritual realm.

Now, the phenomenon of *pay it forward* comes into play. *Pay it forward* is the action for this step, as it is how you maintain the gratitude and humility gained by your work. There is a quote by Ralph Waldo Emerson from his essay, *Compensation*, that sums up this idea: "In the order of nature we cannot render benefits to those from whom we receive them, or only seldom. But the benefit we receive must be rendered again, line for line, deed for deed, cent for cent, to somebody." Paying it forward subscribes to the notion of spiritual reciprocity.

When we find freedom from something that has frustrated and trapped us for so long, the desire to want to tell others takes over. It is the feeling of overflowing, as if you were about to explode with joy and gratitude. I hope you experienced that feeling through the steps of this book. That was my intention.

When we have learned to put ourselves first and value ourselves and our time, it becomes obsessive to share with others. And, if we are clutterers with all the inside and outside clutter, we certainly know others who could benefit.

This next line is key. We mustn't try to force upon them anything we have learned, gained or experienced. Instead, by our actions and changed behavior, we must allow them to see the person we have become.

The truth about the stuff remains true, and the truth about this process is that a person needs to be ready to do the work. They need to be sick and tired of being sick and tired. Not a whole lot is more motivating than pain and discomfort.

I encourage you to share your experience when asked to do so, to spread the message of the positive things you have learned and to share what the experience has meant to you. However, don't make the mistake of trying to tell someone that they *have* to do it. Allow them the dignity to come to their own decisions about what they need to do. No one wants to be told they "need" or "have" to change or fix things.

As these feelings continue to come up for you—and they will—I encourage you to keep filling your journal and sharing your experiences with a trusted friend. Remember that daily spiritual maintenance calls for keeping your spiritual space clean.

I encourage you to share, in a general way, how the spiritual aspect of this process worked for you. Remember that God may be your spiritual guide, but that this may not be true for everyone. We can honor others and their process by respecting the spiritual guide they choose, but if you find someone whose spiritual beliefs and conceptions of God coincide with yours, it can be such a gift to speak freely about how God has changed your life.

Pay it forward action items. Here are a few ideas you can use to pay it forward. You may come up with some of your own and find something that really speaks to where you've been on your own journey.

In the meantime, think about these ideas:

❑ Start a small group and do a gradual clutter clean-up. Spend a few hours or a day helping each other, rotating the meeting place and working together with others who understand how hard this is for you.

❑ Suggest or organize a donation day with your church or community. Encourage others to let go of what's keeping them stuck.

❑ Offer to work with someone else who has just now become willing to look at their clutter problem.

❑ Start a book study group with this book. Work together through the steps and encourage each other. Trade off hosting it so you can come clean with your clutter. Maybe set aside part of the meeting to help each other clean up one small area.

❑ Donate a copy of this book to a friend or women's group where others may have experienced a challenge with clutter.

There are many ways to give back. Get creative. Join forces with a friend. You can be the change you want to see in your own life, and it will become contagious to those around you. People who used to see you depressed and overwhelmed, with your hair on fire, will wonder what you've done when you are looking and feeling better. Peace and serenity are the best accessories to our lives. I can't help but smile when I think about what my life looks like today. Keep up the good work.

Step 5 Summary ~ Share

In this section, we looked at the benefits you gained from taking care of yourself and being willing to put yourself first. You may have struggled with this, but I commend you for your perseverance and willingness. You are making great changes in your life, and I wish you all the best. I would suggest that you now go back to the beginning and start again. I guarantee you will get more, better and different results each time you read this book and do the steps as they are outlined. You can pick a specific situation and do these steps with that in mind, you can also work through with a friend who is also challenged with clutter.

When you have begun to successfully care for yourself and taken the time to clear out some mental and spiritual clutter it makes sense that the external clutter, the physical clutter is less powerful and daunting. I would love to hear from you about your experience, please write to me

My wish for you is that you live the life of your dreams—spiritually, mentally and physically!

In Abundance...

For more information about Kelli Wilson and *The Clutter Breakthrough* you can visit her website at **www.theclutterbreakthrough.com**.

To contact Kelli for personal coaching, clutter breakthrough work groups and speaking engagements you can email her at **inquiry@theclutterbreakthrough.com**.

Notes

Notes